Teaching Listening Comprehension

CAMBRIDGE HANDBOOKS FOR LANGUAGE TEACHERS

General Editor: Michael Swan

This is a series of practical guides for teachers of English and other languages. Illustrative examples are usually drawn from the field of English as a foreign or second language, but the ideas and techniques described can equally well be used in the teaching of any language.

In this series:

Teaching
Listening
Comprehension

Penny Ur

CAMBRIDGE
UNIVERSITY PRESS

Published by the Press Syndicate of the University of Cambridge
The Pitt Building, Trumpington Street, Cambridge CB2 1RP
40 West 20th Street, New York, NY 10011-4211, USA
10 Stamford Road, Oakleigh, Melbourne 3166, Australia

First published 1984
Tenth printing 1992

Printed in Great Britain
at The Bath Press, Avon

Library of Congress catalogue card number: 83–5173

British Library cataloguing in publication data

Ur, Penny

Teaching listening comprehension. –
(Cambridge handbooks for language teachers)
I. English language – Spoken English –
Text-books for foreigners
I. Title
428.3'4   PE1128

ISBN 0 521 25509 0 hard covers
ISBN 0 521 28781 2 paperback

BS

Contents

Contents

Contents

Illustrations

Acknowledgements

This book has benefited from a number of ideas given to me by many different writers, lecturers and colleagues, which I have adapted and used, though unable to remember their original source. To all such unknown contributors – my thanks and apologies.

The author and publishers are grateful to those listed below for permission to reproduce material.
Longman Group Ltd for Fig. 1 (from *What do you think?* by Donn Byrne and Andrew Wright) and the extract from *Meeting people* by Terry L. Fredrickson on p. 93; Edward Arnold Ltd for Fig. 4 (from *The Goodbodys* by Paul Groves, Nigel Grimshaw and Roy Schofield); Munksgaard for the extracts from *Listen then!* by Paulette Møller and Audrey Bolliger on pp. 86, 92, 94–5, 142 and 162–3; Bokförlaget Corona AB for the extract from *Let's listen* by John McClintock and Börje Stern on p. 87; *Punch* for Fig. 13; the *Sunday Express* for Fig. 21; Penguin Books Ltd for Fig. 31a–b ('Chart 13: Production and yields of certain crops in Great Britain' from *Facts in focus* compiled by the Central Statistical Office, Penguin Reference Books 1972, p. 104) Crown copyright © 1972; the producers of *Nature notebook* (BBC World Service) and Prof. J. P. Hearn for the transcript on p. 131; Thomas Nelson and Sons Ltd for the extract from *First Certificate English 4: listening comprehension* by W. S. Fowler on pp. 136–7; Macmillan Education Ltd for the extract from *Points overheard* by Matthew Bennett on p. 146.
Fig. 2 was drawn by Jenny Palmer; the cartoons in Figs. 14 and 15 are by David Mostyn; Figs. 3 and 17–20 were drawn by Trevor Ridley; the other drawings are by Chris Evans.

Part 1 *Understanding spoken English*

This book is about listening comprehension practice in the foreign-language classroom, and is intended primarily for teachers of English. It does not undertake a psycholinguistic, philosophical or communications engineering analysis of the process of listening and understanding; nor, on the other hand, does it consist entirely of a series of exercises. It is, perhaps, an attempt to bridge the gap between the two: to discuss what, in practical terms, successful foreign-language listening comprehension entails; and on this basis to propose types of practice that may be effective in the classroom. Some of these may be found to be suitable for testing purposes also; but their primary aim is to teach rather than to test. I hope that the reader may emerge with some relevant criteria by which to evaluate, select and devise different kinds of exercises.

The three aspects of the subject I shall consider in Part 1 are these: what sort of listening activities actually go on in real life? What are the particular difficulties likely to be encountered by the learner when coping with them? And how may we, as teachers, best help him to master these difficulties?* In other words, we need a clear idea both of where we are going (what we want our students to be able to do as the end result of their learning) and how to get there (what we need to give practice in and how).

---

* The English pronoun system obliges me to choose between 'he' and 'she'. Since I and most of the English teachers of my acquaintance are women, I have chosen to refer to the teacher throughout in the feminine, and the student in the masculine.

1 Real-life listening

At this stage it would be useful if there were available a full-scale taxonomy of all the different kinds of listening situations there are, together with a statistical analysis of their relative frequencies. However, I do not know of any such study – nor am I sure that its execution is at all a practical proposition, since the immense variety of societies, individuals, situations and types of oral discourse must defy classification. On a less ambitious scale, however, it is possible to list some examples of the types of listening we might expect reasonably educated people living in a developed country to be exposed to, and hope that an examination of the results might yield some useful conclusions.

Such a list is set out below, in random order. Not all of the examples are pure listening activities, but all involve some aural comprehension as an essential component of the communicative situation:

- listening to the news / weather forecast / sports report / announcements etc. on the radio
- discussing work / current problems with family or colleagues
- making arrangements / exchanging news etc. with acquaintances
- making arrangements / exchanging news etc. over the telephone
- chatting at a party / other social gathering
- hearing announcements over the loudspeaker (at a railway station, for example, or airport)
- receiving instructions on how to do something / get somewhere
- attending a lesson / seminar
- being interviewed / interviewing
- watching a film / theatre show / television programme
- hearing a speech / lecture
- listening to recorded / broadcast songs
- attending a formal occasion (wedding / prize-giving / other ceremony)
- getting professional advice (from a doctor, for example)
- being tested orally in a subject of study

Now this list is naturally rough and incomplete; nevertheless it is, I think, fairly representative. There are certainly some useful generalizations which can be drawn from it and which have some immediate implications for classroom practice.

1.1 Purpose and expectation

Rarely if ever do we listen to something without some idea of what we are going to hear: only, perhaps, when we turn on the radio or television at random, or enter a room where a conversation is already in progress. Usually we have some preconceived idea of the content, formality level and so on of the discourse we are about to hear. Such ideas are based on what J. C. Richards calls 'script competence', that is the knowledge we possess in advance about the subject-matter or context of the discourse ('Listening comprehension', *TESOL Quarterly* 17:2). Our *expectations* may often be linked to our *purpose* in listening: if we want to know the answer to a question, then we will ask, and expect to hear a relevant response. In many cases this leads to our 'listening out' for certain key phrases or words. When we ask a question like: 'Where are you going to be?', we then listen out for the expression of place. If the answer is, for example: 'I don't know, I haven't really decided yet, it depends what job I get, but I expect I shall end up in Boston' – then we shall wait for and note the last two words. If, however, the same answer is the response to the question: 'Are you definitely going to Boston?' – then the last two words of the answer are virtually redundant, and we shall pay more attention to the first part.

In discourse that is not based on the listener's active spoken participation, his expectations may be less strictly defined, but they are there nevertheless and again are connected with his purpose. If we listen to the news, it is from a desire to know what is happening in the world, and we shall expect to hear about certain subjects of current interest in a certain kind of language. If we are listening to a lecture, we usually know roughly what the subject is going to be, and either need to learn about it or are interested in it for its own sake. If none of these conditions is true then we shall probably not listen at all, let alone understand. Even when listening to entertainment such as plays, jokes or songs, we have a definite purpose (enjoyment); we want to know what is coming next, and we expect it to cohere with what went before.

There is, moreover, an association between listener expectation and purpose on the one hand, and comprehension on the other. Heard discourse which corresponds closely to what the listener expects and needs to hear is far more likely to be accurately perceived and understood than that which is unexpected, irrelevant or unhelpful.

Thus it would seem a good idea when presenting a listening passage in class to give the students some information about the content, situation and speaker(s) before they actually start listening.

1.2 Response

In many, perhaps most, cases the listener is required to give some kind of overt, immediate response to what has been said. This may be verbal (the answer to a question, for instance) or non-verbal (action in accordance with instructions or a nod of the head, for example). Even a lecturer or orator gets some sort of feedback from his audience in the form of facial expression, eye-contact, interruptions, note-taking. Only if the message is coming via electronic equipment when the speaker is neither physically present nor addressing himself to the listener as an individual, is no overt response usually required or forthcoming.

Yet many classroom listening comprehension exercises demand no response until the end of fairly long stretches of speech, so that when it comes this response is very largely a test of memory rather than of comprehension. Occasional exercises like these, and others that demand no overt response at all certainly have their place – I do not mean to suggest that they should not be used at all (see 5.1 *Listening and making no response*) – but on the whole listening tasks should, I feel, be based on short, active responses occurring during, or between parts of, the listening passage rather than at the end.

1.3 Visibility of the speaker

I think it is fair to say that we are nearly always in the physical presence of, or able to see, the person(s) we are listening to. Usually the visibility of the speaker coincides with the necessity for listener-response – but not always. There are cases where we can see the person we are listening to but are not expected to react to him personally (as when we watch a television programme); and there is, conversely, at least one common situation where we cannot see the speaker but must certainly respond to what he says (a telephone conversation).

If the speaker is usually present in real-life listening situations, towards which we wish to train our students in the classroom, then perhaps we should think again about how much we ought to use *recordings* as the basis of our exercises. Perhaps we should revert to using live speakers, resorting to recordings only to attain specific objectives? For a fuller discussion of this question see 3.1, *Using recordings*.

1.4 Environmental clues

Apart from the speaker himself – his facial expression, posture, eye direction, proximity, gesture, tone of voice – a real-life listening situation is normally rich in environmental clues as to the content and implications of what is said. Often noises or smells or other sense-stimuli can contribute valuable background information, but I think it is true to say that most environmental clues are visual. These may be deliberately introduced, as when a teacher or lecturer clarifies her exposition with diagrams or pictures, or a television documentary uses film extracts or stills to illustrate its commentary. Similar clues appear quite naturally in less formal situations, as when someone gives us directions according to a map. Occasionally the general surroundings contribute information: if we are in a railway station, for example, and hear an announcement over the loudspeaker, we expect it to announce the arrival or departure of a train.

Environmental clues are often more likely to provide information about the situation, speakers and general atmosphere than about the actual topic of discourse. If the listener/onlooker cannot understand the meaning of the words used in a family discussion, board meeting or political harangue, he will not be able to say much about the subject of debate. What he will be able to guess fairly accurately, however, are things such as the level of formality, the amount and kind of emotional involvement of the speaker(s), the kind of relationship existing between speaker(s) and listener(s), the prevailing mood – all of which afford him significant assistance in comprehending the sense of what is said once he actually understands at least some of the language. Sound recordings, broadcasts and telephone conversations are relatively poor in such clues, but these normally comprise only a small part of our total listening activity.

In classroom terms, environmental clues are normally represented by *visual materials* (illustrations, diagrams, maps and so on) which are thus essential to the effective presentation of most listening exercises.

1.5 Shortness

Another characteristic of real-life listening is the shortness of the chunks into which heard discourse is usually divided. The usual pattern is a short period of listening, followed by listener-response (not necessarily verbal), followed by a further brief spell of listening with further response, and so on. In other cases, stretches of heard speech are broken up by being spoken by different people from different directions. Even when there are long periods of seemingly uninterrupted discourse – talks, instructions, anecdotes, guided tours, nagging and so on – these are often broken down into smaller units by the physical movement of the speaker, pause, audience reaction, changing environmental clues. More formal stretches of speech – lectures, ceremonial recitation, broadcast reports – are, however, usually less interrupted.

1.6 Informal speech

It is necessary to draw a distinction between formal speech or 'spoken prose' and the informal speech used in most spontaneous conversation. This is not, of course, a simple binary opposition: there are many intermediate gradations, ranging from the extremely formal (ceremonial formulae, some political speeches), through the fairly formal (news-reading, lectures), to the fairly informal (television interviews, most classroom teaching) and the very informal (gossip, family quarrels)*. But for the purposes of this discussion a firm division will be made: any types of discourse which fall more or less under the first two categories I will call 'formal', those in the last two 'informal'. Informal speech is usually both spontaneous and colloquial; formal speech is characteristically neither. Some intermediate types of discourse may be one but not the other: the speech of a character in a play, as delivered by an actor, may use colloquial language but is not spontaneous; and a sermon may be delivered

---

* Compare Joos's five divisions: frozen, formal, consultative, casual, intimate (M. Joos, *The five clocks*, Harcourt Brace, 1967).

extempore but is rarely very colloquial. Broadly speaking, the degree of *colloquiality* of speech affects its pronunciation, vocabulary, grammar and syntax, and the *spontaneity* affects its syntax and discoursal structure.

Most of the discourse we hear is quite informal, being both spontaneous and colloquial in character; and some of the skills the learner needs to develop are closely bound up with the peculiarities of this kind of speech. Of these there are many, but I should like here to dwell on four: redundancy, 'noise', colloquial language and auditory character. Please note that the first two terms are used here rather idiosyncratically, as defined in the two paragraphs which follow.

Redundancy

In ordinary conversation or even in much extempore speech-making or lecturing we actually say a good deal more than would appear to be necessary in order to convey our message. Redundant utterances may take the form of repetitions, false starts, re-phrasings, self-corrections, elaborations, tautologies and apparently meaningless additions such as 'I mean' or 'you know'. This redundancy, however, is not as unnecessary as it would seem. Just as it enables the speaker to work out and express what he really means as he goes along, so it helps the listener to follow him by providing an abundance of extra information and time to think. The message of a piece of spontaneous talk is thus on the whole delivered much more slowly and repetitiously than that of rehearsed, read or planned speech. It is also, as we have previously noted, frequently interrupted by the listener's interpolations, the responses to which may serve as further redundant material.

'Noise'

The opposite of redundancy (extra information) is 'noise', which occurs when information is not received by the listener because of interference. 'Noise', as I am using the term here, may be caused not only by some outside disturbance, but also by a temporary lack of attention on the part of the listener, or by the fact that a word or phrase was not understood because it was mispronounced or misused or because the listener simply did not know it. In any such case, a gap is left which is filled, as far as the listener is concerned, by a meaningless buzz. What the listener has to do is try to reconstruct more or less what the information was that he missed. In an informal conversation he may request

a clarification ('What was that?' 'Sorry, I didn't quite catch
. . .'); otherwise he must just gather up the loose ends as best he
may. This happens a good deal in conversation between native
speakers, and we 'fill in' almost without realizing what we are
doing. Redundancy, of course, often helps us to do this. For
non-native speakers there is far more 'noise' (as defined above)
in heard speech than there is for natives, and it is often difficult
for them to cope with it (for some suggestions on how to give
helpful practice in this, see pp. 84–7, 139–45).

Colloquial language

In most languages there are marked differences between the
formal (or literary) and colloquial varieties. The former is used
not only for written communication but also for all kinds of
formal speech: lectures, reports and so on; whereas the latter is
confined to informal conversation and is rarely written. In
Arabic the difference between the two is so great that children
actually have to relearn their own language when they go to
school. In English, as in most other languages, the distinction is
less marked, but it is there all the same. The sounds a listener
absorbs during a normal conversation bear only a partial
resemblance to a transcript in normal orthography, which in its
turn bears only partial resemblance to a corresponding version
in formal prose. The difference in the first stage is one of
pronunciation; in the second in actual choice of words.

A native speaker may very often not even be aware of the first
difference at all. We may be quite sure that the person addressing us said, for example: 'I don't know; where do you think he
can be?', when what he actually enunciated was something like
'dno, wej'thinkeeknbee' – with no pauses between words, and
less important sounds shortened or eliminated altogether. A
similar sentence pronounced in a formal context would correspond rather more closely to the written form.

The actual vocabulary and structures used will also be
different in some respects from those of prepared texts. The
reader of transcripts of spontaneous conversations is struck, for
example, by the number of occurrences of items such as 'I
mean', 'sort of', 'just', 'you know', which would probably not
occur in prepared speech. There are also some actual changes in
lexis. In colloquial speech we would be far more likely to hear
expressions such as 'a lot', 'get to', 'for ages', 'stuff', 'guy', than
their more formal equivalents 'much/many', 'reach', 'for a long
time', 'material', 'man'. For a discussion of the problems all this
causes the learner, see 2.1 and 2.5.

Auditory character

There is a distinct difference between the auditory effect of a piece of spoken prose and that of informal conversation. The former is characterized by a fairly even pace, volume and pitch. Spontaneous conversation, on the other hand, is jerky, has frequent pauses and overlaps, goes intermittently faster and slower, louder and softer, higher and lower. Hesitations, interruptions, exclamations, emotional reactions of surprise, irritation or amusement, which are all liable to occur in natural dialogue, are bound to cause an uneven and constantly changing rhythm of speech. Even if only one person is speaking for a relatively long period, the fact that he has not thought out carefully what he has to say beforehand, and has not necessarily chosen the best words, means that he has to rely heavily on vocal emphasis to make his meaning clear. And vocal emphasis does not just mean saying a particular word or phrase louder. It means also gabbling quickly through what is less important and slowing down over the main point, or pausing for effect before or after a vital phrase, or raising the pitch of the voice to stress one thing and then lowering it to play down something else. The overall effect of all this is perhaps more dramatic and interesting than that of formal speech, but this does not mean that it is, all in all, more comprehensible or easier to listen to.

To summarize, we may say that most (but not all) of our real-life listening activity is characterized by the following features:

1 We listen for a purpose and with certain expectations.
2 We make an immediate response to what we hear.
3 We see the person we are listening to.
4 There are some visual or environmental clues as to the meaning of what is heard.
5 Stretches of heard discourse come in short chunks.
6 Most heard discourse is spontaneous and therefore differs from formal spoken prose in the amount of redundancy, 'noise' and colloquialisms, and in its auditory character.

Sometimes particular situations may lack one or more of these characteristics – when watching television we are not normally expected to respond, when listening to a lecture we may have to hear uninterrupted speech for a very long time indeed – but it is only very rarely that none of them is present at all. We seldom listen to stretches of 'disembodied' discourse of any length.

What are the implications of all this for listening comprehension in the foreign-language classroom?

It would seem reasonable to say that classroom practice should usually incorporate such characteristics of real-life listening as those described above; yet many books of listening exercises I know do not include *any of them at all*. Such books are often made up of passages originally composed as *written* texts (extracts from novels, newspaper articles and so on) recorded onto tape; the learners listen to the text without knowing much about what they are going to hear or what they are listening for, and then have to answer comprehension questions, usually multiple-choice. This is a convenient classroom technique, and it does give a certain type of practice – but it does not provide any realistic preparation for real-life listening. A learner who relies on this type of exercise is going to have a very rude awakening when he tries to understand native speech in natural communicative situations.

It is not enough, however, to base classroom exercises only on an imitation of reality. We must also take into account the specific difficulties faced by the foreigner in learning to cope with heard English speech.

2 Listening to English as a foreign language

Some aspects of listening comprehension are easier for the foreign-language learner than others. Most learners need intensive practice in some skills and seem to pick up others intuitively. Below are some of the main potential problems, set out roughly in order of importance. In discussing them I have relied heavily on the analysis of spoken English given in Gillian Brown's *Listening to spoken English*; and I refer the reader to this excellent book for a fuller treatment of the subject. For a more detailed taxonomy of the listening skills themselves, see J. C. Richards' article 'Listening comprehension'.

2.1 Hearing the sounds

As a young teacher it took me some time to realize that my students actually did not perceive certain English sounds with any accuracy because these did not exist (at all, or as separate phonemes) in their own language. The sound /θ/ as in '*th*ink' for example does not exist in French; a native French speaker may very often therefore not notice at first that it occurs in English – he may simply assimilate it to the nearest sound familiar to him and both hear and say /s/ or /f/. Even after the distinction has been pointed out to him, and he has practised saying the sound himself, he may continue to confuse it with /s/ or /f/ the moment he starts using the language for something other than pronunciation practice. Even more difficulty is caused when the new sound *does* exist in the native language, but only as an allophonic variation of another phoneme. For example, both /ɪ/ (as in 'pit') and /i:/ (as in 'peep') exist in modern colloquial Hebrew, but they are allophones, and the substitution of one for the other makes no difference to meaning, occurring only because of the location of the sound in the word or sentence. Thus the Hebrew speaker has difficulty in perceiving this difference as significant to meaning in English, and it takes a considerable amount of practice before he gets used to distinguishing between 'ship' and 'sheep' or 'fit' and 'feet'. The distinction between the dark and clear [l] in Russian causes similar problems to the native English speaker.

Sometimes the foreign learner of English may have difficulty with the sequences and juxtapositions of sounds typical of English words. Many students find consonant-clusters particularly difficult to cope with. They may get the consonants in the wrong order (hearing 'parts' for 'past'), or omit one of the sounds ('crips' for 'crisps'), or hear a vowel that is not in fact pronounced ('littel' for 'little').

Another reason why sounds may be misheard is that the student is not used to the stress and intonation patterns of English and the way these influence both the realization of certain phonemes and the meaning of the utterance.

One interesting point about all these difficulties is that it is often quite difficult to know, outside minimal-pair practice, whether students really have heard the sounds right or not, because they may guess the right meaning from the context. In the sentence 'It doesn't fit, it's too big', most students will understand the word 'fit' correctly even though they may have heard it as something approximating to their idea of 'feet'. Is there, then, so much importance in the correct hearing of sounds? Will learners not always be able to understand the word through context, just as they will have to distinguish between genuine homophones like 'meet' and 'meat'?

The answer is yes, there is importance. The number of homophones and homonyms (such as the noun *bear* and the verb *bear*) in English is small, while the number of words which can be confused or misunderstood by inaccurate perception is relatively large. Even if working out what the right word must be takes only a split second, it still slows down comprehension fractionally – and spoken discourse goes by so fast that the foreign listener simply cannot afford a moment's delay. He may sometimes even understand the word according to what it sounds like (to him) in spite of the fact that his interpretation does not fit the context simply because he does not have the time to stop and work it out. It is therefore essential for the learner to achieve familiarity with the common phonemes of the target language as soon as possible if he is to be an efficient listener. I am not concerned here so much with his own pronunciation, but it is certainly true that if he learns to pronounce the sounds accurately himself, it will be much easier for him to hear them correctly when said by someone else.

2.2   Understanding intonation and stress

The English systems of stress, intonation and rhythm, though perhaps less obviously difficult than problems of the actual sounds, can interfere with the foreign learner's proper understanding of spoken English. It is, therefore, worth drawing our students' attention to the existence of certain general patterns. Primary among these is the division of utterances into *tone-groups* – strings of syllables run together to form a single sequence and generally characterized by one heavily stressed 'tone'. The rhythm of speech is based on these 'tones' and to a lesser extent on other minor stresses, and intervening lightened syllables may be pronounced very fast so as not to break this rhythm. It takes roughly the same time to say 'the CAT is INterested in proTECTing its KITTens' as it does to say 'LARGE CARS WASTE GAS', though the number of syllables each sentence contains is very different (examples taken from the article 'Listening comprehension' by J. C. Richards); whereas in most other languages, twice as many syllables simply take twice as long to say. As to *intonation*: its importance derives from the great extent to which it often influences the meaning of an utterance: a significant word is often stressed simply by being pronounced in a higher 'key', for example; and such things as certainty, doubt, irony, inquiry, seriousness, humour, are implied by characteristic intonation patterns as much as by choice of words.

Having demonstrated some of the standard patterns, we can usefully do some classroom exercises whose object it is simply to sensitize students to their existence (see pp. 37–45). Beyond this, I do not think there is much useful teaching to be done in this field: the stress, intonation and rhythm patterns of spoken English are so varied, so idiosyncratic and so unpredictable that it would be of dubious value to give or practise any more detailed models. Having, as it were, pointed our students in the right direction, it is probably best to leave them to acquire intuitively more detailed knowledge through exposure to plenty of informal native speech.

2.3   Coping with redundancy and 'noise'

When listening to someone speaking, we usually have to put up with a certain amount of 'noise'. Some words may be drowned by outside interference, others indistinctly pronounced. The foreign-language learner, whose grasp of meaning is slower than that of a native and demands more of an effort, finds these gaps far more difficult to take in his stride. He is, it is true, used to coping with them in his own tongue, but when he has to do the same in another language, he finds he cannot do so with anything like the same facility. This is for three main reasons. First, the sheer number of gaps is much larger: there are some items he cannot understand simply because he does not know them, many others which he is not yet sufficiently familiar with to grasp during rapid speech (though he could probably recognize them if faced with them in writing or in slow, carefully pronounced formal talk). Second, he is not familiar enough with the sound-combinations, lexis and collocations of the language to make predictions or retroactive guesses as to what was missing. A native speaker, for instance who hears only /sprin/ can guess that the final phoneme will be /t/, making the word 'sprint'; or if he hears the phrase 'He was in a towering . . .', he can predict that the last word will be something like 'rage'. But a learner cannot normally be expected to have the information necessary to enable him to guess in this way (for further discussion of the practical implications of this, see pp. 16–17). Third, even when the number of gaps is not much larger than those they would encounter in their own language, many foreign-language learners run into a psychological problem: they have a kind of compulsion to understand everything, even things that are totally unimportant, and are disturbed, discouraged and even completely thrown off balance if they come across an incomprehensible word.

It is this third problem – the apparent need of the foreign-language learner to perceive and comprehend everything he hears even though he would not do so in his native language – whose significance is not always realized. In the early stages of foreign-language learning, when the learner hears usually only single words or short sentences, he has to understand them all. Later, listening comprehension passages get longer, but in most cases (unless the teacher is aware of the problem and adapts her material accordingly) they are still graded to suit his level, taken slowly and pronounced carefully, and he is still expected to understand everything. He assumes that successful comprehension is total comprehension, and finds it very difficult to get used to the idea that he can be a perfectly competent listener with less than 100 per cent perception and/or understanding of what is said. The same phenomenon, incidentally, occurs in reading. A learner who is at the transition stage from intensive to extensive reading also has to learn to grasp the meaning of a sentence even when it includes a word or two he does not know. The reader, however, has the advantage of time: he can stop if he wishes and try to make an intelligent guess as to the meaning of the missing items. The listener has to take the gap in his stride and be satisfied with the rough idea conveyed by the rest of the utterance, or hazard a quick intuitive conjecture.

A foreign-language learner who tries to understand every single word that is said to him will be handicapped both by his failure to do so and also, in a way, by his success. On the one hand he is distressed and discouraged by his 'defective' comprehension, has the feeling that he has missed vital words, and may tell you 'I didn't understand a thing' when in fact he has, or could have, understood quite enough for communicative purposes. On the other hand, even if he does perceive and understand every single word he hears, he may find this actually counter-productive: for effective listening is aided by the ability of the listener to ignore or 'skim' unimportant items. Much of what we hear is redundant, and we have to recognize it as such. We need – and have, in our native language at least – a mechanism which tells us: 'I don't need to listen very carefully to what is coming now, it's obviously going to be more or less "x"'. For example, if someone says: 'You don't need to meet my train; if it's raining then perhaps yes, but if not . . . ' then it does not really matter if the last few words are going to be 'don't bother' or 'I can walk' or simply 'don't'. The listener can safely 'switch off', more or less, and look forward to what is coming next. The foreign-language learner who listens carefully for the exact sense of such redundant phrases and attaches importance to it is actually hampering himself. He is not taking advantage of a natural rest or break in the stream of significant information in order to ready himself for what is coming next, nor is he sorting out significant from insignificant content as he goes along. He is concentrating very hard – too hard – on understanding the words or phrases as they come up, and not relaxing enough to gather the main message. He is in danger, as it were, of not seeing the wood for the trees.

The ability to make do with only a part of what is heard and understand the main message is a vitally important one for effective listening in a communicative situation. It is a mistake to think that this ability will be automatically carried over from the native language. Once the learner has moved over from intensive to extensive listening in the foreign language and got used to coping with 'noise' and recognizing redundancy, his own native language skills will come into play; but he needs conscious practice in making the transition (see 5.3, *Filling gaps* and *Summarizing*).

2.4 Predicting

If the listener can make a guess as to the sort of thing that is going to be said next, he will be much more likely to perceive it and understand it well. He may even be enabled to do without it altogether: if he knows, that is, how someone is going to finish his sentence, then the closing words become for him redundant, and he will be able to 'skim' or even ignore them and start anticipating the next significant piece of information, as in the example given on p. 15.

Prediction is difficult for the foreign-language learner for various reasons. Intonation and stress patterns play an important part in supplying ground for certain kinds of expectations. If one word in an introductory phrase is emphasized, for instance, we may usually expect some sort of explanation or amplification of it to follow: 'I don't mind her seeing *John* . . .' (It's *Ned* I don't want her to see) or 'No, no, we're going by *train* . . .' (Train's much faster). A sentence pronounced with a marked intonation of doubt is usually followed by a strong reservation: 'Of course he's a very pleasant boy . . . ' (*But* . . .) or 'Well, I suppose they might come . . .' (*But* . . .). As we have seen in 2.2, the subtleties of stress and intonation are difficult to teach; and prediction exercises may be one of the best ways of getting students used to hearing the semantic implications of certain patterns.

Other predictions may depend on total familiarity with the clichés, collocations, idioms and proverbs commonly used; a non-native speaker cannot usually be expected to know that 'rosy' often collocates with 'cheeks' or 'jaded' with 'appetite'; nor can he automatically supply the end to such cryptic phrases as 'People who live in glass houses . . .' or 'A stitch in time . . .'.

However, most predictions do not depend on such subtleties but on more obvious choices of vocabulary or grammar. For instance, the use of 'but' or 'however' makes us expect something contrasting with or opposing what went before; the use of a conditional verb such as 'would have' often precedes or follows an 'if' clause; to begin a sentence with 'the more . . .' implies another paired comparative later; and obviously an introductory clause such as 'There are two reasons for this' signals a corresponding discourse structure to follow. In short, a learner who has a reasonable grasp of the pronunciation, vocabulary and grammar of the foreign language may often be expected to make the same prediction of what is to follow as a native speaker, aided only by skills he carries over from the use of his own language. However, he sometimes needs some encouragement and practice to take full advantage of these skills in the context of the new language.

Some exercises on predicting may be found in 5.3, *Predictions*.

2.5 Understanding colloquial vocabulary

Much of the vocabulary used in colloquial speech may already be known to the foreign listener; but this does not mean that he is familiar with it. This may look like a contradiction, but it is not; and, like the subject treated above, it is one which is often overlooked. It is fairly obvious that a learner listening to spoken discourse in the foreign language will probably not understand a word he has not learnt yet. What is not so obvious, but nevertheless true, is that he will also fail to recognize many words he *has* learnt but is not yet sufficiently familiar with to identify when they occur within the swift stream of speech.

This is partly a matter of time and practice. Mastering new items to the stage of total familiarity is a very gradual process: it takes time before a newly learnt word becomes really known well enough to be readily recognized. It is partly a question of speed of discourse. The overall pace at which a message is conveyed may be relatively slow owing to pauses, hesitations and so on, but once a (native) speaker knows what he is going to say next, his individual utterances are often delivered at a tremendous rate. The listener simply does not have the time to search his memory for the meaning of something he does not immediately recall.

The learner also needs to know that certain expressions are common in colloquial English and more or less taboo in formal style; some examples have already been given in 1.6, *Colloquial language*. But actual lexis is the least of the problems here and one which can easily be overcome if the teacher is aware of the necessity of teaching the extra items together with the limitations on their use. Far more subtle difficulties are posed by the different pronunciation of known words or of colloquial collocations.

When a student learns a new word or expression, he usually learns both its written and spoken form. His recognition of it is linked to his knowledge of what it looks like on paper and what it sounds like when carefully pronounced, whether in isolation or – usually well 'foregrounded' – in context. But he has not, often enough, learnt what it sounds like when said quickly, in an unemphasized position in a sentence and juxtaposed with other words which may affect its pronunciation. If a word is pronounced differently in informal speech from the way it is said formally, or was said when it was learnt, the listener may simply not recognize it as the same word, or may even miss its existence completely. This problem can be defined as one of vocabulary as much as of pronunciation, since the foreign-language learner, in my experience, assimilates many of the new forms as fresh, variant lexical items. He seems to learn that 'don't' means 'do not' in very much the same way that he has to learn 'a lot' for 'much'. Chief culprits here are the frequently occurring small function words like 'for', 'to', 'him', 'is', and 'has', which, when unstressed (as they usually are), are heard as /fə/ (American English /fr/), /tə/, /ɪm/, /z/, /z/: the so-called 'weak' forms.

Some words may disappear completely. 'Where are you going?' may quite acceptably be pronounced exactly like 'Where you going?' without a grammatical mistake being either made or heard. Even more confusing for the foreigner is the occasional disappearance of an apparently vital negative: witness the sentences /ðeɪːˈɑːʔˈgəʊɪŋ/, /aɪˈkɑːʔˈkʌm/ ('They aren't going', 'I can't come'), where an almost imperceptible hesitation or slight glottal stop (represented here in transcription by the symbol ʔ) takes the place of the negative 'n't'. Of course, the native speaker knows that were the sentences positive the auxiliary verbs 'are' and 'can' would be pronounced differently by most people – but how is the learner supposed to know that? He expects to hear the negative word as he has been taught to say it himself.

Longer words too may be pronounced differently from the foreign listener's expectation not because of their placing in the utterance, as in the examples above, but because their normal colloquial pronunciation does not accord with their spelling. Often the vowel in an unstressed syllable is shortened or changed. Such a vowel may sound like /ɪ/, as in /dɪˈsaɪd/ ('decide') or /ˈmænɪdʒ/ ('manage'); more commonly it may be reduced to the neutral vowel sound or 'schwa' (/ə/): /kənˈtrəʊl/ ('control'), /ˈfæməlɪ/ ('family'), /ˈpensəl/ ('pencil'). In some cases, vowels may disappear altogether: such words as /ˈvedʒtəbl/, /ˈcʌmftəbl/, /ˈsekrətrɪ/ ('vegetable', 'comfortable', 'secretary') are often very difficult for foreigners to decode.

Sometimes the juxtaposition of two words means that one of the sounds at the junction point has assimilated to the other or even disappeared: /ˈtemˈpiːpl/ for 'ten people', /sɪˈdaʊn/ for 'sit down', /ˈɔːˈraɪt/ for 'all right', /ˈsteɪpmənʔ/ for 'statement'. In any case, the result is sufficiently removed from the original expected sound of the words in question to confuse the foreign listener: he may think there is only one word where there are two or more, or fail to recognize a perfectly familiar item. Even if such confusion causes him only a moment's hesitation, the delay may be fatal – enough to make him miss the next few sounds and lose the thread of the message.

Colloquial collocations are most confusing of all. There are certain pairs or groups of words which tend to occur together and become so merged that both speaker and (native) listener relate to them as a single item. The effects described on pp. 17–18 are even more marked in such expressions, as the component words shorten, slur, distort and partially assimilate to one another. The learner may soon get used to such well-known and consciously-taught combinations as 'can't', 'he's', 'we're' and so on; but what about /'wɒtʃə/, /də'nəʊ/, /'wɒsə/, /'gɒnə/, /ʃwiː/ for 'what are/do you …?', 'I don't know', 'What's the …?', 'going to', 'shall we …?' – all of which commonly occur in the speech of perfectly well-educated clear-speaking natives? It is hardly surprising that in varieties of English based only upon spoken, colloquial language (pidgins), many such collocations have been treated as, and become, single words in their own right. For the learner, such phenomena take some getting used to, and it is essential for the teacher to be aware of their existence and the problems they cause.

For some suggestions for practice, see 4.2.

2.6 Fatigue

Anyone who has learnt a foreign language knows how tiring it is listening to and interpreting unfamiliar sounds, lexis and syntax for long stretches of time. Reading, writing and speaking are also tiring, but at least as far as these activities are concerned, the learner can set his own pace and make breaks where he wishes. In listening, the pace is set by someone else, and the breaks may or may not occur where the listener needs them. Also, as remarked on p. 14, many foreign-language learners seem to work much harder than necessary aiming for accurate perception and interpretation of every word they hear.

The effects of fatigue vary a great deal, depending on how hard the learner needs to concentrate and on his ability to do so for long periods. But it is certainly a fact that in a long listening comprehension exercise a learner's grasp of the content is much better at the beginning and gets progressively worse as he goes on. This is partly due to a psychological phenomenon (we tend to perceive and remember the first of a series of visual or aural stimuli better than we do later ones); but it is also very largely because of fatigue: the listener runs out of the energy necessary to absorb and interpret the strange sounds.

2.7 Understanding different accents

Many foreign-language learners who are used to the accent of their own teacher are surprised and dismayed when they find they have difficulty understanding someone else. Some of them try to get over this at first by claiming that the second speaker's accent is somehow inferior or 'wrong'. But strictly speaking there is rarely such a thing as a 'wrong' accent: there are simply accents that are more or less difficult to understand – that is, broadly speaking, ones that are more or less removed from the original variety learned. We must remember also that the English many of our students will need to understand may very well not be spoken in a native accent at all. Today, two people who do not speak each other's language will very often use English as the instrument of communication: pilots communicating with ground control, for example, diplomats negotiating, businessmen making deals, or anyone at all concerned with the tourist industry . . . and only a minority of these may be native speakers. Hence, even if we could teach all the 'native' accents there are, this would not satisfy many learners' needs. What we can do is try to give them a reasonable familiarity with the two most useful English accents – that is to say, the British and American standard varieties – and then perhaps let them have a taste of some others simply to open their eyes to the possibilities and give them some practice in coping with them. Learners who have some experience in listening to and understanding a number of different accents are more likely to be able to cope successfully with further ones than those who have only heard one or two.

2.8 Using visual and aural environmental clues

Many foreign-language learners seem to lack the ability to use environmental clues to get at the meaning of an imperfectly grasped phrase: time and again I have come across instances of students who have misunderstood something because they are analysing words in isolation and not linking them to the context or accompanying visual stimuli. They may, for example, understand 'horse' for 'house' in spite of an illustrating picture, or sit down when I say 'come here' in spite of a gesture of invitation.

What is the problem? There is certainly no question of the students being unable to perceive and interpret visual or other stimuli as such – they do so perfectly well in their own language. Thus I see no value in practising this skill in isolation: exercises such as listening to a conversation in order to discover how many participants there are, or watching a film extract and describing the emotions or relationships of the actors – these may be fun, and the intellectual student may enjoy analysing how he comes to his conclusions, but they do not improve his ability to understand foreign discourse in context.

For the problem is not the lack of skill in perceiving and interpreting extra-linguistic clues, but the ability to *apply* it when listening to the foreign language. And the reason why the foreign-language learner has difficulty here would seem to be because his receptive system is overloaded. He has to work much harder at decoding than the native listener and, as described on pp. 14–15, tries to interpret every detail as it comes up instead of relaxing and taking a broader view. He simply does not have the time and attention to spare for absorbing information beyond the actual semantic significance of the words themselves.

These difficulties will not be overcome simply by drawing the learner's attention to the presence and importance of environmental clues; on the contrary, such action is liable merely to increase the number of details he feels he has to take in, and make him even more strained and frustrated. What we need to do is encourage him to relax, gather what he can from the information he can readily decode, and use his common sense and the discourse skills he carries over from his native language to help him understand the whole. Exercises aimed at training students to skim for specific information, to ignore details and gather general import, to cope with redundancy and 'noise', and to listen for recreation and pleasure (see Part 2) – all these encourage a relaxed, holistic approach to the understanding of heard discourse and may therefore provide the best means of helping to free the foreign listener to perceive and exploit all available clues to meaning.

3 Planning exercises

When planning listening exercises it is essential to bear in mind the kind of real-life situations for which we are preparing students, and also the specific difficulties they are likely to encounter and need practice to overcome. But we also need to take into account a further complex factor: the nature of the classroom teaching–learning process itself. There are physical considerations such as the size and arrangement of the classroom, or the number of students; technical ones such as may be involved in the use of tape recorders or other equipment; and a mass of pedagogical ones: how to improve student motivation, concentration and participation; how to correct, or give feedback; how to administer exercises efficiently, and so on. As a practising teacher, I am constantly exasperated by the lack of attention paid by many materials writers to such aspects of the language teaching–learning process; exercises that look lovely on paper often do not work in practice simply because some obvious feature of classroom practice has been overlooked. It is these practical features which in the last resort determine whether an activity will do its job effectively or not.

What I shall try to do in this last chapter of Part 1 is to combine the theoretical considerations discussed in previous chapters with the practical factors mentioned above in order to outline some characteristics of the kind of listening exercises that will give maximally effective and relevant practice in the classroom.

3.1 Listening materials

Producing suitable discourse

Many listening comprehension exercises used today in the classroom are still based on formal spoken prose, in spite of the fact that, as we have seen, most heard speech is in fact spontaneous and colloquial in character. There is, it is true, a certain amount of spontaneous teacher-talk in the foreign language in the course of other language-learning activities (explanations, instructions, comprehension questions), and much of it provides incidental listening practice. But this is not enough; and listening comprehension exercises as such are usually based on a text prepared in advance and read aloud by the teacher or on tape, which obviously does not give the kind of practice needed. Theoretically, there is no justification for this. In practice there is very good justification indeed: that it can be very difficult technically to plan and administer stretches of spontaneous speech, whether live or recorded.

The use of recordings of authentic unrehearsed discourse has two main drawbacks. First, being authentic, the speech used in such recordings is ungraded and the language is often very difficult, suitable only for the highest levels. Second, anyone who has listened to recordings of natural conversation knows how difficult they are to understand; without seeing the speakers it is very hard even for a native listener to disentangle the thread of the discourse, identify the different voices and cope with frequent overlaps. These two disadvantages together mean that sound recordings of authentic conversations have only limited value as bases for listening exercises. Video-tapes might be better, and may provide some useful practice for high-level learners – but relatively few institutions have the facilities, and even when these are available, their use often entails a daunting amount of planning, coordination, timing and technical preparation on the part of the teacher. In any case, the problem of the relative difficulty of such material remains. Some authentic material can of course be adapted for classroom use, but usually only after careful selection and editing.

If we abandon the idea of using recordings of authentic conversations as basic texts, then we must also abandon our attempt to achieve complete spontaneity, because obviously as soon as people start thinking about how they are going to sound, and about the words they are using, they will not be quite spontaneous.

But is complete spontaneity so necessary? Does hearing authentic discourse really provide the best training for real-life listening? I would say not. Students may learn best from listening to speech which, while not entirely authentic, is an approximation to the real thing, and is planned to take into account the learners' level of ability and particular difficulties.

With regard to recorded material: if the texts are carefully enough graded, prepared and administered, then the final transition from 'imitation' authentic to 'genuine' authentic speech should take place smoothly. There may be various degrees of approximation to authenticity. We can have easy written texts read aloud with as natural a rhythm and pronunciation as possible; or we can use texts deliberately composed in colloquial idiom and read as nearly as possible as if they were being made up on the spot. We may have our speakers embroider a skeleton text or notes, using their own words but controlling the difficulty of the language. Finally, we can give only a basic situation, and invite speakers to improvise their own interpretation – guiding or editing if necessary.

If listening material is presented 'live' then it is of course much easier to control the level of difficulty and formality (for a discussion of the relative merits of recorded and 'live' discourse, see *Using recordings* below). The teacher can take the information she wants to convey to the class and deliver it in her own words, simplifying and slowing down a little perhaps to suit her students' level, but providing nevertheless a reasonable model of spontaneous natural speech. Teachers who are experienced, native speakers, and well acquainted with their students can do this fairly easily; but those who lack one or more of these attributes may have difficulty – or think they have. They may feel uneasy about improvising, unsure if they are speaking correctly or using an appropriate variety of the language, they may be tense and hesitant . . . in short, they often feel much happier if they have a text in their hands to read.

Reading from a text is an easy way out that should be avoided if possible. Spontaneity is far more important than accuracy; and in any case, students who learn from native English speakers do not necessarily seem to acquire noticeably better accents than those who learn from non-natives. Any teacher with a reasonable command of English can improvise listening material in the classroom (if she cannot, she should not be teaching English anyway), and should make a conscious effort to do so as often as possible. Some advice on doing this can be found on pp. 47–51.

Using recordings

It seems to be taken for granted these days that listening practice should be based on (cassette) recordings; and sometimes one has the feeling that this assumption is encouraged for reasons irrelevant to their actual efficacy, such as the financial interests of the people who produce them, or our own odd illogical guilt-feelings: 'If we *can* use up-to-date electronic equipment, then we *ought* to'! Let us look objectively at the pros and cons.

Taped listening passages can be prepared in advance, thus saving the teacher work in the actual lesson. When the teacher's pronunciation is noticeably foreign, recordings may provide the students with some valuable exposure to native accents; and their use also makes available a far greater range of language situations: different voices and accents, moods, registers, background effects. Moreover, it may seem rather difficult for a single teacher to present *dialogue* effectively in the classsroom using only her own voice – a recording can solve this problem. Finally the absence of a visible speaker forces the students to focus on the actual sounds, thus·giving more concentrated aural practice.

On the other hand, as we have seen, the speaker is actually visible to the listener in most real-life situations, and his facial expression and movements provide some material aids to comprehension, so that it does not seem right to consistently deprive the learner of his presence in classroom exercises. Also, if the speaker is (as is generally the case) the teacher herself, then she can adapt the material as she goes through it, varying, pausing and repeating parts to suit the needs of her students. A further disadvantage of recordings is their technical quality: even professionally-made tapes are not always as distinct as they should be, and their clarity may be further impaired by faulty or inferior playing equipment. Finally there is the inconvenience of getting, bringing and setting up the recorder, plus the occasional hitches that go with the use of any automatic machine.

The obvious conclusion is that both recorded and live speech should have a place in classroom exercises. However, to my mind live speech does on the whole seem to be a more useful and practical basis for practice and should be used more often, particularly if the teacher can bring other English speakers into the classroom. Recordings should be used for definite specific purposes: to make available types of discourse, accent or listening situations that are difficult to present live, to make students concentrate on aural perception of the foreign sounds, intonation or stress patterns, or for testing.

3.2 The task

As a general rule, listening exercises are most effective if they are constructed round a task. That is to say, the students are required to do something in response to what they hear that will demonstrate their understanding. Examples of such tasks are: expressing agreement or disagreement, taking notes, marking a picture or diagram according to instructions, answering questions.

A pre-set purpose

In real life when we listen to someone talking we have a definite non-linguistic reason for doing so. In the classroom the genuine reason for listening is purely linguistic (to improve the students' listening skills), and a non-linguistic purpose has to be consciously superimposed in the form of a task. The task is in fact the realization of the twin ideas of purpose and expectation in practical classroom terms. If the learner knows in advance that he is going to have to make a certain kind of response, he is immediately provided with a purpose in listening, and he knows what sort of information to expect and how to react to it.

Ongoing learner-response

The task also provides a framework for immediate response by the listener which as we have seen on p. 4 is a characteristic of most listening situations. Intermittent listener-responses also have the effect of breaking up the heard discourse into 'gobbets', more naturally and easily perceived and absorbed than long stretches of unbroken speech.

However, classroom realities do not allow us to simulate typical real-life responses. For example, the typical real-life response to a spoken stimulus is a spoken reply – but obviously no teacher can cope with a classful of students all giving their own individual spoken answers at the same time, let alone check and correct them. If we want all the students to perform the task and their results to be available for checking, then most of the responses will have to be silent: action, marking, drawing or writing.

However, tasks that involve a lot of reading (such as answering multiple-choice questions) or writing (such as taking notes) have one disadvantage that should be noted. There is a huge difference between the time taken to understand heard information (and draw conclusions from it), and that taken to read possible paraphrases or write one's own. Even many native speakers find it quite difficult to do multiple-choice listening exercises or make notes from lectures simply because of this problem; and when all is said and done, such exercises probably do more for the written skills than for listening. At later stages, when listening is being practised together with the other skills in general fluency activities, these exercises come into their own; but if we want to concentrate on aural comprehension itself, it is best to base the task on easily grasped visual material (pictures, diagrams, grids, maps), and quick simple responses such as physical movement, ticking-off, one-word answers.

Motivation

It is much more interesting to respond actively to something than to listen passively; and a well-constructed task can be fun as well as learning-effective, for an element of puzzle-solving or game-playing is easily built in. The topic of the task too can contribute to the interest and enjoyment generated by the activity. In lower-level classes selecting topics is not so much of a problem since the vocabulary available limits the range to subjects such as the family, the house, animals, the body and so on. Later, however, the students' command of language allows a much wider selection of topics. Here we must try to avoid boring or over-theoretical subjects, using as far as possible ones we think our students may be interested in, that seem of practical relevance, that may arouse or stimulate them. A little drama or humour can do a great deal towards arousing interest even if not of a particularly high standard of sophistication! For some examples of varied tasks and topics see Part 2.

Success

Tasks should be success-oriented. This not only improves motivation (if students succeed in one such task they will be so much more willing to tackle another) but also ensures the effectiveness of the listening practice given. Listening exercises are meant to train not to test; and the best practice is obtained by having learners do the activity more or less successfully, not by having them fail. Thought should be given to appropriate grading both of the language and of the task type so that they are not too difficult. Giving material that is too easy is, in my experience, much less of a problem; it does not seem to happen so often, and even when it does, no harm has been done – the class still gets its (slightly less valuable) listening experience, whereas exercises that are too hard give little practice and can actually cause harm by frustrating and demotivating students.

The task itself should always be relatively easy and the focus remain the listening itself; once students understand the language they should be able to do the activity as a whole with no difficulty. If the task is too hard, time-consuming or complex then the actual listening comes to take up a relatively small part of students' time and attention and the amount of listening practice afforded is correspondingly small. This is a common fault to be found in published task-centred exercises, where far too much is often demanded of the student in terms of memorizing and comparing different items of information or complex logical inference. However, if the teacher tries out such exercises on herself or on a colleague before presenting them in class, such defects usually reveal themselves, and alterations can be made to correct them.

Simplicity

The preparation and administration of the task should also be as simple as possible. Beware of activities involving too many bits of paper, items of equipment or separate stages; they may take so long to prepare and set up that the practice achieved is just not worth the investment: the exercise is not cost-effective, so to speak.

Feedback

Students should be given immediate feedback on their performance of the task. Reading and writing assignments, in contrast, can tolerate delayed teacher-feedback to a greater degree. If a student has done a written exercise or answered comprehension questions on a reading passage, the teacher's reactions may safely be delivered a day or two later; the students can always reread the relevant material in order to understand and appreciate the teacher's comments. Speaking and listening, however, need to be reacted to immediately. It is obviously absurd for the teacher to correct a mistake in a student's speech a day later, and even to wait a minute or two may cause the comment to lose some of its relevance. The same applies, in slightly less extreme fashion, to listening. If a student does a listening task such as checking a list or answering questions and is then given back his answers with corrections a day or two later, he will reap very little benefit from the feedback given. His recollection of the actual words he heard will be hazy, and he has no means of knowing exactly where and why he went wrong. His results need to be checked immediately he has finished, when what he has heard is still echoing somewhere in his mind and there is still a possibility of hearing it again. I usually give the correct results first, thus allowing students to assess their own performance, and then go through the entire exercise again, explaining as I go, so that they can understand their mistakes and learn from them. There is another factor involved here as well – that students *want* to know the correct answer immediately they have done a task, are frustrated if it is delayed, and may very well lose some of their interest by the time it does appear (motivation again!). But the chief argument is certainly the pedagogic one: the learning value of listening exercises is increased if there is immediate teacher-feedback on student performance.

Lack of a task element may impair the effectiveness of the listening practice given. Take for example the conventional activity that consists of a recorded listening passage followed by multiple-choice comprehension questions: it has no specific pre-set task and no necessary ongoing responses; it places an unnatural load on students' memory and provides little interest or challenge; nor does it simulate or give preparation for any real-life listening situation that I can think of. For these reasons such activities are perhaps not a very good vehicle for listening practice as such. This however does not invalidate them as classroom techniques – as tests, for example (see 5.3, *Answering comprehension questions on texts*).

However, there is at least one type of listening activity that does give effective practice without the help of a task. When the material itself is so interesting or pleasure-giving that it holds the students' attention and demands their understanding for its own sake, the setting of a task becomes superfluous or even harmful. Such material may be contained in a good story or song or in a film or play in the foreign language, or simply in informal anecdotes, opinions, or general interesting chat improvised by the teacher (see 5.1).

3.3 Visual materials

Contextualization

Some environmental, usually visual, accompaniment to heard discourse is a characteristic of most listening situations as we have seen on pp. 5–6. In the classroom these environmental clues will usually be represented by different kinds of visuals: pictures, sketches on the blackboard or overhead projector, flannel- or magnet-board cut-outs, objects. The presence of such materials is of immense value in contextualizing and bringing to life the listening situation as well as in aiding comprehension of the language. I would go so far as to say that some kind of visual clue is essential in any language-learning activity based on face-to-face communication.

Learning and motivation

Visuals have an important function as aids to learning, simply because they attract students' attention and help and encourage them to focus on the subject in hand. It is relatively difficult to concentrate on spoken material that is heard 'blind', far easier if there is something relevant to look at. If this something is conspicuous, colourful, humorous, dramatic or in motion – so much the better: striking and stimulating visual aids are likely to heighten students' motivation and concentration. The teacher can be her own visual aid, of course, by acting or miming – but there is such a thing as overdoing it. I have known students so entertained by the antics of their teacher that they were actually *distracted* from what was being said!

Pictures and diagrams as task-bases

A distinction must be drawn between *visuals-based* exercises and *visuals-aided* ones. In the latter, the visual may appear in the form of one big poster, and provides information on which the teacher can base the listening text; whereas in visuals-based exercises, each student has his own copy of the material and uses it not only to get information but also as an answer-sheet on which he is to mark his responses to tasks, such as noting inconsistencies, filling in missing items, making changes and so on. Examples of visuals-aided tasks can be found in the first seven sections of 5.2 *Listening and making short responses*; visuals-based tasks appear in the last six sections of 5.2.

Visuals-based exercises are interesting to do and potentially very effective, so recently published listening-comprehension books usually include a number of examples. The trouble is that an illustration once marked cannot usually be used again, so that constant use of books like these can become expensive. For this reason I use a lot of home-made materials duplicated on the school's copying machine, keeping my designs as simple as possible. Some basic sketches can be duplicated en masse and then used for many different purposes (see 5.2 *Ground-plans*); and even very detailed materials can usually be exploited in more ways than one.

PICTURES

Picture-based activities are suitable on the whole for younger learners. Pictures used should be clear representations of objects, people and scenes whose description is more or less within the lexical range of the class. They should include enough detail and variation to allow for plenty of description and imaginative elaboration. Black-and-white cartoon-type sketches are best as they are usually very clear and easily reproduced.

DIAGRAMS

I am using the word *diagram* here in a slightly wider sense than is usual, to denote any representation of information in diagrammatic form – not just graphs or family trees, but also maps, plans, tables and so on. Older students are usually familiar with diagrammatic conventions and can 'read' such material readily. The advantages of diagrams as bases for task-centred activities derive from the fact that they (diagrams) are designed to convey a large number of facts clearly and quickly without necessitating a heavy load of reading. Hence one simple diagram can generate a large amount of language to explain, describe or comment. Moreover, diagrams can represent information on a wide variety of topics and express many different relationships, so that much more varied subject matter is made available than would be possible using only pictures. An excellent selection of diagrams suitable for English teaching can be found in the books *Cue for a drill* and *Cue for communication* by Shiona Harkess and John Eastwood.

Both pictures and diagrams should be simple enough to be grasped at a glance. Over-detailed pictures are confusing and difficult to scan. Complicated diagrams are even worse: faced with elaborate graphs or maps students will have to spend some minutes working out what it all means before they can even begin to think about listening, and will also be delayed during the listening passage itself finding their way about the material in order to make appropriate responses. Similarly, any writing on a diagram should be kept to a minimum. Simply drawn symbols with lines to show relationships between them are quickly grasped; reading words takes much longer. A few isolated written words, it is true, are almost inevitable in many diagrams, but full sentences should be avoided.

Like the over-complex tasks described on pp. 27–8, over-elaborate visuals occur frequently in published task-centred listening exercises. The teacher is advised to check this point carefully before presenting such exercises in class.

Part 2 Suggestions for classroom activities

Understanding foreign speech is a complex activity involving a large number of different skills and abilities. It follows from this that classroom listening practice is also complex, and that no one type of exercise – nor two, nor half a dozen – can possibly satisfy the needs of most foreign-language students. The teacher should therefore have at her fingertips a large battery of different exercises designed to give practice in most, if not all, of these various skills. Moreover, listening should be practised very frequently, so that such exercises will be in constant use. This is not quite so time-consuming as it sounds. Most listening activities suggested here can be easily adapted so that they practise lexical, grammatical, or functional–notional material that is being learnt anyway in the class. Many others are very short – taking two or three minutes each – and require little or no preparation.

Because of the large number of exercise-types suggested, I have found it convenient to organize them into subordinate categories arranged in a rough progression from the quicker and simpler ones at the beginning to the longer and more complex ones at the end. Chapter 4 comprises different kinds of *Listening for perception* exercises where the main objective is simply to train the learner to perceive correctly the different sounds, sound-combinations and stress and intonation patterns of the foreign language. Chapter 5 is composed of a number of different kinds of *Listening for comprehension* exercises, ranging from very 'passive' ones, where the learner simply listens, making little or no response, to very 'active' ones, where the listening is only the preliminary to or basis for more sophisticated activities involving other language skills and imaginative or logical thought. This division is not meant to represent a strict chronological order of application in the classroom; variations of most types of exercise can, in principle, be used at any level of proficiency.

Part 2 is not intended essentially as a classroom textbook, though I hope that much of the material may be usable as it stands: it is rather a taxonomy of different exercise-types. The materials and presentation of each such exercise-type are described in detail, with examples, and notes are appended giving information on suitable published material and instructions or suggestions to help teachers prepare their own.

4 Listening for perception

The main aim of this type of exercise is to give the learner practice in identifying correctly different sounds, sound-combinations and intonations. It is the only category where actual comprehension is a secondary consideration, the emphasis being on aural perception. Thus, in most of the examples, visual and contextual clues to meaning are eliminated or kept to a minimum in order to induce the learner to rely upon his ear. The exercises are made up of short discrete items; this is partly because we want to isolate and concentrate on the particular sounds that need practice, partly because in long passages contextual clues come into play, and the learner does not have to rely on the accurate aural perception we are aiming for. Such items may be responded to by the learner in various ways: he may be asked to reproduce them orally, identify their written form, translate, and so on. All such tasks are simple and quick to do.

At what stage in the learner's progress in the foreign language should these exercises be used? It seems obvious that a grasp of the phonology of the new language is a fairly basic requisite for learning to speak it, and that therefore these exercises should be used right from the start. However, at least at the very early stages, many learners do not yet read the language well enough to be able to use written words as a basis for sound-practice; they may not know the Latin alphabet at all, or they may associate the letters with the corresponding sounds in their own language. Early training will therefore have to be based on purely oral–aural work without using written material at all. Later, the use of written forms makes possible a wider range of exercise-types.

It is a good idea to use recordings rather than live speech here. Again, this forces the learner to rely on his ear alone; it also gives the teacher greater scope in the use of different voices and accents.

Under 4.1 *At word-level* I shall deal with exercises that practise different sounds and sound combinations which occur within single words; whereas 4.2 *At sentence-level* is concerned rather with the problems that arise when words are put together

35

to make sentences: the distortion of sounds within common collocations, unclear word-division, intonation, and so on.

4.1 At word-level

At the early stages students need practice in hearing and saying the sounds of isolated words as they are ideally pronounced by a native speaker, without the distortions or blurs which commonly occur within the context of natural speech. At this level, the listener's main problem is simply to identify the right phoneme(s) and hence the right word.

Learning new sounds is not a particularly intellectual activity: it is more a matter of acquiring habits. The process of teaching them, therefore, is mostly based on a behaviourist model. The teacher demonstrates the sounds she wishes to teach and encourages students to imitate or identify them. When she feels they are hearing and reproducing them with a fair degree of accuracy, she gives them a series of tasks whose purpose it is simply to familiarize them with the new sounds to the point where they can identify, if not pronounce, them accurately, easily and without hesitation. It is important to remember that the object of such exercises is to *train* not to test: if students are consistently getting wrong answers, then the practice is useless, and the teacher should stop, demonstrate again the sounds she wishes to teach, and make sure her students have grasped them before continuing. Checking and correcting by the teacher should therefore take place at frequent intervals, possibly after every item, and certainly not only at the end of an entire exercise.

Should we use 'mock' English or real English words for perception exercises like this? If students do not know the meaning of the words, they are more likely to use their ears carefully, instead of guessing from what they think they 'ought' to be. For example, I have had students understand 'pen' when I had said 'pan', because they had learnt the meaning of the first item and not of the second. On the other hand, this very mistake derives from a listening strategy we are going to want to *encourage* – that is, guessing what something is likely to be even if it has not been perceived properly. And neither students nor teachers really like practising with nonsense words; we prefer using real words even if their meaning is of no importance. Perhaps it is best either to give only rare words, and make sure the students are aware of the fact that they have not learnt them yet, or give them known words, where the words with which they are likely to be confused are also familiar.

One final point: sound-perception practice should be provided using a variety of techniques, so that the students (not to say the teacher!) do not get bored with what is, after all, a fairly mindless, if essential, part of the language-learning process. A varied selection of such exercises is suggested below.

Oral activities

REPETITION

Students with accurate aural perception can often reproduce sounds they hear without having the slightest idea what these mean. However, the more complex the material to be reproduced, the more difficult it is to repeat it accurately without understanding. For the purposes of this category of exercises, therefore, repetition should be based on short, easily memorized words. The teacher says, or plays on the tape recorder, a word or two, asks individual students to repeat them, and corrects where necessary. Having to imitate the sounds themselves helps learners to hear them correctly; but it must be remembered that mispronunciation does not necessarily imply that they are hearing them wrongly; students can often clearly perceive subtle distinctions they are incapable of reproducing themselves. However, where the distinctions are fairly clear and merely need to be pointed out and practised, repetition can be a particularly valuable exercise. For example, in practising consonant-clusters (as in *string, risks, gentle, comfortable*), learner-repetition can help the teacher make sure that the sounds have all been heard in the right order and without 'extra' vowels.

Repetition is rather time-consuming. It takes a long time to hear an entire class repeat a single word, while most students are silent and relatively inactive most of the time (in small classes, of course, this objection is less serious). Some useful practice may be obtained by the use of pair-work (two students take turns imitating words dictated by a tape recorder), or choral responses; but in neither case does the teacher have much direct control over the quality of the results or much opportunity to correct.

ENGLISH OR NOT?

After teaching a new sound, the teacher contrasts it with the nearest equivalent in the native language, and then asks the students to identify which is which. The best way is to give a word which exists in similar form (not necessarily meaning) in both languages, and ask students to say from which language a particular pronunciation of it comes. For example, the teacher might contrast the German *er* with English 'air', or the French *il* with English 'eel'. The students hear one of each pair and identify the right language by calling out, marking a tick in a labelled column in their notebooks, or by raising right or left hands. They do not need to understand the English words, but only to identify them as English.

Lists of sounds that tend to be confused between English and most other widely spoken languages can be found at the end of *Introducing English pronunciation* by Ann Baker, but the actual sets of words used for exercises like these will have to be compiled by the teacher. It is best to stick to common, short words at least at first in order to 'foreground' the particular sound being practised.

WHICH CATEGORY?

Another categorization exercise which does not involve writing is based on the difference between two sounds *within* the foreign language. These can be identified by number: the vowel in 'man' for example can be called *one*, and that in 'men' *two*. The teacher then calls out 'pen, cat, rap'; the students say or note down *two, one, one*.

SAME OR DIFFERENT?

Again using minimal-pair distinctions, the teacher calls out two words and challenges the students to say if they are the same or different; they could, for example, write down a tick if they think they are the same, a cross if not.

Similarly, the teacher can call out a series of three or four words and ask the students to say which, if any, is the odd one out, identifying again by number. The teacher says, for example, 'pin, pin, bin, pin,' the students say *three*; or, practising the order of sounds: 'cast, carts, cast, cast'.

HOW OFTEN DID YOU HEAR IT?

The teacher gives short phrases or sentences and asks students how often they heard a particular sound; for example, she can ask them to listen out for the sound /ɪ/ as in 'ship' and say 'Read it in the magazine' or 'a bit of cheap ribbon'. It is important to tell students what to listen out for *before* they hear the phrase.

Reading and writing activities

When the students can read the foreign language at a minimal level – that is, they know what letters or letter-combinations usually correspond to what sounds – exercises can be devised that use the written forms as a basis. The same exercises, incidentally, can be useful as reading and writing practice, particularly for students who have had to learn an entirely new alphabet.

IDENTIFYING THE RIGHT WORD

The class is given duplicated sheets consisting of sets of two or three words with minor auditory differences between them – these differences being based on the sound or sound-distinction that the teacher wishes to practice. The teacher then dictates (herself, or using a recording) one word from each such set, which the students have to identify by marking in some way (circling, underlining, etc.) Not more than two or three words should be given each time, because if there are more, some students may not be able to scan them all quickly enough to identify the right one in time.

The number of such sets of words given at one session varies of course with the age and level of the students. For young children at the elementary stage, five or six is enough; and even advanced students should not be asked to cope with more than ten or twelve straight off, since identifying foreign sounds requires a lot of concentration, at least at first. At the early stages, when the students have only just begun to learn the sounds, the 'right' words can be demonstrated several times, with pronunciation slightly exaggerated to make sure they are identified correctly. Gradually they come to be pronounced more naturally and repeated less, until the sounds are being recognized fairly easily.

A variation of the above can be administered using the same sets of words. In this, the teacher reads out both, or all three of the words in each set – but in an order which may or may not differ from that in which they are written down. The students have to number the words in the order in which they have heard them. This looks more difficult than the previous exercise, but the basic identifying process is in fact easier, since the students can hear the contrasts and use them to differentiate.

Similarly, students can be given only one written word and asked to identify it out of three spoken ones. For example, they might have before them the word 'but', and hear three numbered or lettered options thus: 'A bat B bet C but'. They then write the appropriate letter beside their word.

WRITING THE RIGHT WORD

If the student is familiar with the sounds of the foreign language and their correspondence to conventional written forms, then he should be able also to write out a reasonable phonetic representation of words he hears using the conventional alphabet. A series of words can be dictated and the student asked to write them down. Or he can be given a list of words with one or two letters missing in each, and be requested to fill them in to correspond with a spoken version.

Being able to write down a 'reasonable phonetic representation' is not, of course, the same as being able to spell correctly, owing to the complex and often unpredictable nature of English orthography. The exercises described here are not, therefore, to be confused with conventional dictation exercises, and misspellings are treated as 'wrong' only if they do not accurately represent what was said. If the teacher gives the word /piə/, for example, she must be willing to accept the forms 'peer', 'pere', 'pear' and 'pier' – but not 'pir' or 'per'. Since this might seem to be encouraging bad spelling, it is, perhaps, simpler to limit the sounds we ask students to write down to ones that are more or less invariably represented by certain letters, such as /d/, /t/, /p/, /b/, /e/, /æ/. It is particularly useful to use writing, like oral repetition, to help students practise listening to words where there are unnatural (for them) juxtapositions of sounds. If they have to reproduce the sounds in writing then they listen carefully to make sure they have heard them right (combinations such as s*pr*ing, a*ng*le, and nasally exploded ones such as bi*tt*en, di*dn*'t and so on).

Meaning-based activities

If a student can interpret correctly the meaning of a spoken word then he has probably heard it correctly; so that checking understanding would seem to be a good way of checking accurate perception.

Meaningful words for perception practice have to be given in isolation, otherwise the student may guess their meaning from the context without necessarily perceiving them rightly. He may also guess at their meaning simply on the basis of words he knows, again without accurate hearing: he may, for example, as suggested on p. 36, mistake 'pan' for 'pen' simply because he knows the latter word and not the former. A third problem about identifying meaning in listening perception exercises arises because normally a student's knowledge of the phonology of a language is ahead of his knowledge of its lexis – in other words, an elementary or intermediate student does not normally know the meanings of enough words to supply many examples for minimal-pair practice. Take, for example, the fairly popular exercise where the student is presented with juxtaposed pictures of, say, a bird and a beard, and asked to identify which corresponds to which heard word. It seems to me that most students who are so advanced as to know the meaning of 'beard' will probably also have a sufficiently good grasp of the sound-system not to need this kind of practice. (However, this may not be true of speakers of certain foreign languages (Japanese, for example) who have particular difficulty with English sounds; and exercises such as these may also supply useful practice for students who have attained a high degree of proficiency in the written language without much exposure to the spoken.)

In general, the best kind of meaning-based perception exercises are those using minimal-pair discrimination, where only one of the pair need be a lexical item well known to the students. The meaning of this one is given, by graphic representation or by translation, and the students asked to say to which spoken word it corresponds. Thus, in the above example I would give only the picture of a bird, or the students' native-language equivalent, dictate 'A bird B beard' and hope that the students would say or write 'A'. More than two items can of course be used (one could add 'C bed' to the above).

Lists of minimal-pairs and further material for exercises can be found in *Ship or sheep?*, *Tree or three?* and *Introducing English pronunciation* by Ann Baker, to whom I am indebted for many of the ideas given above. Other books containing useful material for this type of exercise can be found listed in the *Bibliography* at the end of the book.

4.2 At sentence-level

Once words are integrated into sentences within colloquial, spontaneous speech, recognizing them becomes far more difficult. Some of the specific problems for the foreign learner have been described in Part 1 (2.1 to 2.5 inclusive): the contraction and even disappearance of weak forms or unstressed syllables; assimilation or elision of consonants; ill-defined word-division;

distortion of the component words in common collocations. In practice, all these factors combine to produce what Gillian Brown (*Listening to spoken English*) calls an 'acoustic blur', out of which the listener has to try to reconstruct what words the speaker actually meant. Most native speakers are unaware of the imprecision of articulation in everyday English speech: hearing something like 'sh'we go?', a native listener is likely to be sure he has heard the /l/ in 'shall', and will need considerable convincing before he accepts that he has not! As teachers, however, we must be aware of what is happening, so that we can understand the difficulties of our students and help them get over them. We can do this by exposing them to many examples of 'blurred' utterances and teaching them to recognize what these represent. At first, of course, such utterances should not be presented within extended authentic-style discourse, but as isolated instances, with perhaps slowed delivery and some indication by the teacher of what has in fact happened to the sounds. As students get used to understanding such forms, these can be presented faster and integrated into longer stretches of speech.

Oral activities

REPETITION

Students are asked to repeat short phrases or complete utterances said by the teacher or recorded. If they have understood what component words were intended, they are likely to repeat the utterance in 'ideal' form, thinking that this is what they have heard: you say something like 'd'no', they say 'I don't know'. This is good in one way, in that it indicates they have recognized and disentangled the words. But on the other hand, if we want to sensitize them to the kind of 'blurring' that takes place, it may be a good idea to insist on a more accurate imitation of the spoken version; this will also, of course, help them towards a more natural-sounding pronunciation of their own. Thus there are in fact two kinds of repetition exercise which can usefully be done here: translation into 'ideal' form, and exact (or near-exact) sound-reproduction.

For such exercises it is important not to let students see the written version of the heard material, otherwise they will not have to rely on their ears to interpret what they have heard. Also, a written version often interferes with accurate perception: if the students see a 't' at the end of 'don't', it will be that much more difficult to convince them that they did not hear it.

As suggested in the introduction to this section, the models presented at first should not be embedded in long sentences or grossly slurred, but given in short 'chunks' with only the most basic changes from the 'ideal', and slightly slowed down. It is quite difficult at first to get used to slowing one's delivery while retaining the shortenings and distortions characteristic of fairly rapid speech; but this is a useful skill to cultivate, since it can be very helpful to learners trying to grasp a rather confusing sequence of sounds to hear them initially presented less rapidly.

Repeating models of intonation and stress patterns is also a useful exercise: again, students tend to hear the sentences as they think they 'ought to be' pronounced, and can benefit from having the inaccuracies in their own imitations pointed out and corrected. The perception (and production) of *unstress* is even more difficult than that of stress, and needs a lot of practice; intonation is, for most learners, easier to grasp.

IDENTIFYING WORD-DIVISIONS

One way of giving students practice in identifying word-division correctly is to ask them how many words there would be in the written form of a given utterance. For example, you say something like 'wotcha won?', they recognize this as the spoken version of 'What do you want?', and write 4. This can very usefully be done with phrases such as those given on p. 46, which can be presented as they stand, or, for slightly more difficult work, embedded in longer sentences.

Reading and writing activities

IDENTIFYING STRESS AND UNSTRESS

Students can be asked to mark on a written text where they think the stressed or unstressed words are. It may be useful for them to try to do this at first without hearing the spoken text, and then check their conjectures against the latter afterwards. In short utterances it is fairly easy to mark stresses; what is more difficult, but no less important, is to indicate unstress. I suggest that stresses be marked using underlining or accents, unstresses with brackets (students should not be asked to mark both stress and unstress in the same exercise). Here is an example:

Basic sentence: I'm terribly tired; I think I'll go and have a rest.
Stress: I'm térribly tíred; I thínk I'll gó and have a rést.
Unstress: (I'm) ter(ribly) tired; (I) think (I'll) go (and have
   a) rest.

Such exercises can, of course, be done orally – the students repeat the stressed or unstressed words only – if the teacher wants a quick minimal-preparation drill. For more careful and thorough practice, however, it is better to use an accompanying written text as indicated.

IDENTIFYING INTONATION

Again, students are given a written list of sentences or phrases, listen to them being spoken, and mark the intonation they hear over the appropriate words. This is probably most easily done using arrows:

What did you say? Yes, I know.

Intonation is usually borne by the stressed words: so it helps if students have done some work on stress before going on to practise intonation.

DICTATION

The kind of rough phonetic representation using the convention-al alphabet which is recommended on p. 40 for practice of 'ideal' word-forms is not suitable here. We are using longer sequences of sounds, with less carefully defined pronunciation, and students would find it tedious and difficult to reproduce them in writing in this way. At this stage, therefore, we revert to the normal 'dictation', using conventional orthography. This means that we have no way of ascertaining whether students have perceived the sounds exactly as we said them; but it does mean that we can judge if they have understood and interpreted them correctly. The dictation is thus the written equivalent of the type of oral repetition defined above as 'translation into an "ideal" form'.

For *listening for perception* purposes the dictation should not be based on a passage of formal prose, but, like all the other exercises suggested here, on short utterances, possibly, but not necessarily, cohering to form a dialogue or monologue.

Meaning-based activities

If we are concentrating on giving students practice in perceiving accurately, and therefore understanding, discrete utterances, then probably the quickest and neatest way of checking they have in fact understood is by asking for a native-language translation, either orally or in writing. Any of the material used for other exercises in this section can be used here too. But this, of course, can be done only if the teacher knows the students' native language; otherwise, students can be asked to match sentences to pictures or questions to answers: here the material needs to be more carefully selected.

But a picture that illustrates a sentence rather than a word will probably depict a situation, not just a 'thing'; and question–answer sequences are the beginning of discourse-level rather than sentence-level language. At this stage listening skills other than accurate aural perception are coming into play, and the emphasis is gradually shifting from *listening for perception* to *listening for comprehension*.

All the exercises suggested in 4.2 *At sentence-level* are based on sets of short utterances which may or may not be combined into short dialogues or monologues. Some useful material of this type, planned to serve as a model for perception and pronunciation practice, can be found in Ann Baker's *Ship or sheep?*, and in other books listed in the *Bibliography* under *Listening for perception*. Otherwise the teacher can make up her own material, draw ideas from her textbook, or use recordings of listening comprehension passages. Most listening comprehension recordings, however, are either in very formal style (in which case they do not illustrate many of the phenomena we want to practise), or, if approximating to authentic everyday speech, they are often too fast, and too continuous and overlapping to be conveniently dissected into suitable short 'chunks'. One publication which can be used for these exercises is *Variations on a theme* by Alan Maley and Alan Duff. This is composed of a series of brief dialogues, mostly in the colloquial idiom, whose individual utterances can be presented singly for interpretation, and later recombined into the original conversations for more advanced work. The teacher can either use the recording, or read aloud the transcriptions herself. However, if she does the latter, she must be careful to pronounce the sounds in a naturally 'slovenly' fashion! The temptation when reading aloud is to say the words as they are written.

As well as practising listening to such material in order to get used to the acoustic forms of spontaneous speech in general, it is worth devoting a little time to listening to specific, common, colloquial word-combinations where the shortenings, and occasional distortions together with a high speed of delivery make it particularly difficult for the learner to disentangle the components. I have found no published list of common English collocations whose spoken forms are hard to identify or pronounce native-fashion: so here is a list of my own together with a phonetic transcription, which represents one of several 'fast colloquial' RP realizations. It is far from exhaustive, but the teacher may find it useful as a basis for practice:

Spelling	*Sound*	
let's have	'letsəv	
I'll be (going)	ʌbɪ('gəʊɪŋ)	
got to	'gɒdə	
he doesn't like it	ɪ'dʌzn̩'laɪkɪʔ	
there isn't any	'ðrɪzn̩denɪ	
and so on	ən'səʊwɒn	
excuse me	'skjuːzmiː	
you shouldn't have	juː'ʃʊdn̩dəv	
more and more	'mɔːrən'mɔː	
I'm going to	əŋ'gəʊɪntə	
I want to see it	ə'wɒnə'siːɪʔ	
you and me	'juːən'miː	
a lot of	ə'lɒdə	
I don't know	də'nəʊ	
as usual	z'juːʒl̩	
I'd better(go)	ə'bedə('gəʊ)	
what do you (mean)?	'wɒdjə('miːn)	'wɒtʃə ('miːn)
you know	jə'nəʊ	
he doesn't	ɪ'dʌzn̩ʔ	
tell him, tell her	'telm̩, 'telə	
what does he (want)?	'wɒtsɪ('wɒnʔ)	
where's the (boy)?	'wezə('bɔɪ)	
how are you?	hɑ'ːjuː	
wasn't it?	'wɒznɪʔ	
what are you (doing)?	'wɒtʃə ('duːɪŋ)	
don't you?	'dəʊntʃə	
quite a long ...	'kwaɪʔlɒŋ	
what have you got?	'wɒtəvjə'gɒʔ	
just the same	dʒəsdə'seɪm	
you can (get)	'juːkn̩('geʔ)	
you must(come)	juːməs('kʌm)	
can't go	'kɑːʔ'gəʊ	
all right	'ɔː'raɪʔ	
where are you (going)?	'wejə('gəʊɪŋ)	

5 Listening for comprehension

In this chapter I suggest a number of types of exercise that conform on the whole to the guide-lines laid down in Part 1: that is, they give useful preparation for real-life listening, provide practice in some specific aspects that are problematic for learners, and are straightforward to administer and interesting to do in the classroom. Of course, not all the activities conform to these principles to an equal degree: one may concentrate on practising a specific skill at the expense of enjoyment or real-life relevance; another may give good practice but be difficult to administer. But all in all I hope that the exercise-types will be found to be of a wide enough range and variety to cover the above-mentioned elements satisfactorily.

The chapter is divided into four parts: the first comprises exercises where the learner simply listens without necessarily making any overt response; in the second, a minimal (usually non-verbal) response is required to demonstrate understanding; in the third, the responses are more extensive and may involve reading, writing and speaking, and some thinking-out of problems; in the last, listening takes its place as only one (albeit fundamental) skill used in fairly demanding fluency- and study-tasks. There is a general progression from easier, simpler activities at first to more sophisticated ones at the end; but many of the exercises will be found to be appropriate to very varied levels of proficiency and different age-groups.

At least one example of each exercise-type is given in full. The accompanying text is written out in prose style with only token approximation to the spontaneous spoken mode I recommend in general. This does not mean that the text is meant to be read out in the classroom as it stands, though it can be; it is presented in this way simply to facilitate reading – exact transcriptions of spontaneous speech tend to be rather irritating and tedious to read. If the teacher wishes to try these exercises out herself, she should, in most cases, re-improvise her own text. The dialogues, which have no accompanying recording, may seem to present a particular problem: how does one teacher alone deliver them? However, I generally find it quite feasible to read or semi-improvise them to a class without much changing of voice or acting, provided I say the name of one speaker clearly before his or her speech, and pause before saying the next. Alternatively, some of the dialogues may be recast as monologues, or recorded as they stand with the help of another English speaker.

As regards additional ideas for actual exercises: where there are good listening comprehension books available using similar techniques I have given full references in the bibliography. Where I know of no such published material I have made some attempt to supply a number of further suggestions of my own. Such further suggestions are not usually given in the form of complete texts written out. Their content is indicated either through graphic representation or in the form of notes which the teacher can use as a basis for improvising the discourse.

Improvising from skeleton notes is very easy to do, but there are one or two points over which the teacher must take care if the improvisation is to succeed. First, she must make quite sure in advance that the notes or illustrations are easily comprehensible to her, so that she will not suddenly have to stop to puzzle out what is meant. Second, she must be aware that improvising informal discourse from notes does not just mean embedding the content in full sentences, giving a sentence to each item of information. If she does this, she will find that the resulting text will be far too concentrated, lacking the redundancy typical of spontaneous speech, and that students will have trouble keeping up and doing the listening task, particularly if the latter entails, as often recommended, a series of ongoing active responses. Thus, content given in note form must be expanded much more than at first appears necessary, using plenty of elaboration, repetition, rephrasing, 'phatic' interpolations ('well', 'you know'), comments, clarifications, appeals to the listeners ('Did you get that?' 'Are you with me?'), pauses, hesitations etc. Doing all this actually makes the improviser's task much easier, as well as resulting in a natural-sounding text that gives useful listening practice.

Here are two examples of what I mean. In each, the notes or graphic material is given first, followed by the transcription of a teacher-improvisation derived from it. In the first, a sequence of events is expanded into a story; in the second, the teacher identifies faces by description, using the portraits as a basis:

1 The fox and the geese

Hungry fox found six geese in field.
Wanted to eat them – said so.
Goose begged for last favour – to say prayers.
Fox agreed.

Geese cackled prayers loudly.
Farmer heard, came, chased fox away.

Once upon a time there was a fox. And this fox was very very
hungry. He hadn't eaten for a long time, and he was just dying for a
good meal. So . . . he went out of his wood and walked towards a
farm where he knew there were some . . . geese and chickens and
ducks. In a field near the farm the fox came upon a flock of
beautiful fat white geese. They didn't hear him coming, and when
he got really close they suddenly heard him and realized that they
were trapped, they couldn't get away, the fox was going to eat
them. 'I'm going to eat you!' said the fox threateningly. The geese
were absolutely terrified, they didn't know what to do, and they
begged. . . . But one of the geese who was a little cleverer than the
rest turned to the fox and said: 'Well, Mr Fox, you've got the better
of us this time, you're obviously going to eat us, we have no way of
escape. Can we please ask one last favour?' Well, when the fox
heard this, and he was so sure the geese couldn't get away, he
decided he'd give them one last favour, and he said: 'All right, one
last favour you can have. What do you want?' The goose said:
'Erm . . . I'd like to say my prayers.' And this seemed a reasonable
request to the fox, so he said: 'All right, you can say your prayers,
but get a move on . . . I'm hungry.' He sat down and the geese
began to say their prayers. Well, when geese say their prayers
they say them in very loud cackles, and they opened their mouths
and cackled and cackled and cackled as loudly as they could, while
the fox sat and listened and thought: 'What a terrible noise they
make saying their prayers.' Well, the noise of their cackling could
be heard as far as the farmhouse, so what do you think happened?
The farmer of course heard the cackling, knew something was
wrong, picked up his gun, rushed out of the farmhouse, rushed
down to the field and there he saw the fox. At the same moment the
fox saw the farmer and of course he . . . had no time to eat any of
the geese, turned round and ran away as fast as he could back to
his wood, as hungry as when he had left it that morning.

2 See the pictures in Fig. 1.

Right . . . you can see in the picture some people talking on the
telephone. Some of them are happy, some of them are serious,
some of them are sad . . . old . . . young . . . men . . . women. I'm
going to talk about three of them, see if you can identify which is
which. O.K. The first one I'm going to talk about is Tom. Tom is a
young man, and he's wearing some kind of dark jacket. He has
short hair, it's difficult to tell if it's dark or fair. Tom has obviously
had some good news, or perhaps he's talking to his girlfriend or
someone he likes very much, because he's smiling, looks very
pleased and happy. That's Tom. The next one I'm going to talk
about is Kate. Kate of course is a girl, or woman, not very old. She
has hair which is not very short, but also not very long, and Kate

Fig. 1

doesn't look happy at all. She looks very serious, perhaps someone is telling her some bad news. She isn't actually talking, she has her mouth shut, and she's listening to someone talking to her. The third one I'm going to talk about is Bob. Bob is an older man. He doesn't have much hair any more . . . and he's wearing a suit. He looks rather worried, very worried in fact, obviously trying to talk about some problem which is rather difficult for him to solve and worries him. O.K. That's Bob.

I am indebted for the ideas in this section to the work done on the subject by Ron White and Marion Geddes and reported in their article 'The use of semi-scripted simulated authentic speech and listening comprehension' (*Audio-visual Language Journal*, 16:3). For further workable examples of skeleton stories see *Once upon a time* by John Morgan and Mario Rinvolucri.

5.1 Listening and making no response

Having made a point of explaining in Part 1 that most of what we hear we also respond to, it may seem rather perverse to recommend at this point a series of no-response exercises. But there are certainly many real-life situations where we do not respond; and in the classroom such exercises have at least one big advantage: if we do not have to keep stopping to hear and give feedback on our students' responses then we have correspondingly more time for the actual listening itself, and can get through a great deal more material. Thus, no-response exercises can be an excellent framework for exposing students to relatively large amounts of spoken English, providing much of the sheer quantity of listening experience needed for optimal learning.

But if there is no response, we need other ways of ensuring that students are actually listening – it is no use providing them with hours of spoken material if they do not absorb any of it! The text, and its presentation, must be particularly geared to attracting and holding students' attention: it should not be difficult; its content should be pleasing and interesting; and if possible it should be delivered 'live' and accompanied by graphic or written materials that provide a visual focus and give help in understanding. Whether, after all this, students are actually listening or not can be fairly well judged by a glance at their faces. Optionally, the teacher can also throw in occasional native-language clarifications (for the weaker students) or questions (to 'jog' the more apathetic ones).

The first two exercise-types discussed here involve the use of written or memorized texts and therefore do not provide optimal conditions for aural practice. However, they are useful as an easy preliminary to activities where the learner does have to concentrate on his listening skills, such as hearing descriptions of visuals or teacher ad-libbing, or listening to songs, stories or plays – as described in the last three sections of 5.1.

Following a written text

Listening to a text and reading it at the same time is something that is frequently done in the foreign-language classroom: the teacher reads out a story or question, and the students follow her words in their textbooks. This is certainly a valid technique for presenting new material and aiding reading; and it does get students used to how the language sounds and to the correspondence between orthography and pronunciation. But beyond this, such activity has only limited value for training in listening comprehension. It does not help to develop learners' reliance on their ear, since the written form is there to give the answer in cases of doubt. Also, it does happen occasionally that the written word actually interferes with accurate aural perception. For example, if a student reads the words 'all right', he is less likely to perceive that the spoken form has in fact been /'ɔː'raɪʔ/, and fails to 'absorb' that form for future recognition. Finally, the use of a written text (unless this is a transcription of speech) often precludes the use of colloquial style.

No particular material is recommended here; obviously any written text can be used in this way.

Listening to a familiar text

Most of the exercises in this book are based on material that the student is hearing for the first time. The reasons for this are fairly obvious: we rarely in real life know exactly what we are going to hear (though we usually have some general expectations); listening to a familiar text does not demand such intensive exercising of the perception or comprehension skills, since the student knows more or less what it is all about without listening carefully; and lastly, the teacher has no way of assessing quite how good the student's listening comprehension was if he (the student) knew the content and meaning beforehand. However, hearing familiar material certainly has value as a sort of easy transition between listening for perception and listening for comprehension, or between listening as a supplement to reading (as described above) and listening as free communication. When the student hears something he is simultaneously reading, he may not need to use listening comprehension skills very much – he can always fall back on the written text. When listening to material he knows by heart on the other hand, he does at least have to rely on his ear; yet once he has perceived the sounds, understanding is much easier than grasping totally new material, and the listener is more relaxed.

Dialogues are good bases for this type of listening: the text is learnt by heart by the students and then listened to as spoken by native speakers. If longer texts are used – short stories, poems, songs – then the student may not know every word by heart, and he will use the spoken or sung words as clues or reminders – one step further in the progression towards free communicative listening.

This kind of exercise is obviously very easy to administer, with no task or teacher-assessment involved. It simply gives plenty of easy and pleasant experience in listening to meaningful English sounds. But this easiness itself can be misleading: students may think they are listening and understanding effectively when in fact they are only recognizing what they knew already; and they may get a rude shock when they realize how difficult it is to understand a listening passage of comparable difficulty which they have *not* studied before. It is important, therefore, not to dwell too much on such practice, but to use it only as a transition to exercises based on unfamiliar texts.

As to material: 'bits' suitable for learning by heart can often be found in the classroom textbook. Dialogues short enough to be learnt by heart can be taken from *Variations on a theme* by Alan Maley and Alan Duff or *Ship or sheep?* by Ann Baker. For songs see the last section of 5.1, *Entertainment*.

Listening aided by visuals

In this type of exercise, learners look at visual material while simultaneously following a spoken description of it. The latter may be limited strictly to details that can be verified visually – or it may include extra information, using the illustration as a jumping-off point for longer narrative, description or discussion. The discourse is easily improvised using the visual material as a basis.

A simple, large, clear drawing can be used, put up on the board or projected using an overhead projector; or a number of small pictures can be distributed among students. In either case, all the students have to do is follow the spoken description according to its graphic representation, looking at the various components of the latter as they are mentioned. In spite of the fact that they do not actually seem to *do* anything much, I have found that students usually concentrate very well in an exercise of this sort. If the teacher wishes to make quite sure her students are following properly she can ask them to point at the relevant parts of the illustration as they listen.

PICTURES

The descriptions can simply be based on what is seen around: the classroom environment. Or the teacher can describe a particular object in the room (a vase of flowers, a magazine, a clock, an item of clothing), or a member of the class. But of course such possibilities are quickly exhausted, and really *pictures* are the most practical basis for simple graphic description.

For fairly elementary classes, we might use a picture like that shown in Fig. 2, and its description could run something like the following:

You can see the picture of a park somewhere in a town. You can see it's in a town because there are some big houses behind the park. Two women are sitting on a bench; one of them has black hair, and she's giving some food to a pigeon – the other woman is just looking at it. Three more pigeons are on the ground nearby. Then there's a man with a little bag in one hand – I think he's got pigeon food in it, because he's throwing food to the pigeons and they're eating it. On the path there's a little boy playing with a hoop and running away towards the entrance of the park. Behind the path you can see the statue of a man with a tall hat sitting on a horse; and there are some flowers growing around. There are two trees in the picture, on either side of the statue.

Fig. 2

A series of different pictures can be used for a similar type of activity. Here, the student has to identify which picture is being talked about as he listens. Here is a description of the pictures in Fig. 3 (intermediate level):

Mark is about fifty years old, not a very popular person, he always seems to be cross about something. He's rather shortsighted, but is said to be quite a good doctor.

Doris is rather a serious type. She's about twenty-five, very attractive, and dresses beautifully.

Then there's Pam, she's a cheerful little thing: long hair which she wears in plaits with ribbons, and freckles on her nose.

Finally there's old Jake. He used to be a sailor, past it now. But he still wears his sailor's cap. He's about seventy and has a beard.

Fig. 3

Supposing we take a strip cartoon, or picture story, and the teacher tells the story rather than describing the pictures. In this case, the students follow the narrative, linking the events to the corresponding drawings. They may, optionally, be asked to point to the right pictures to show they know where the story has got to.

The pictures in Fig. 4 are taken from *The Goodbodys*, by Paul Groves, Nigel Grimshaw and Roy Schofield. The accompanying story might run as follows (easy intermediate level):

Fig. 4

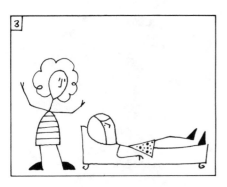

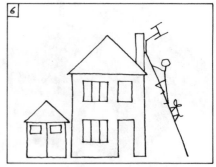

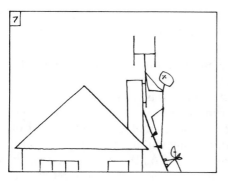

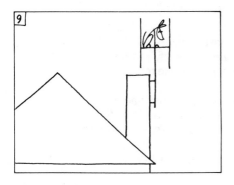

Yesterday Mum wanted to watch television, but when she turned it on, she found it wasn't working. All she could get was some wavy lines. She asked her husband if he could do something about it, but he was busy reading his newspaper and smoking his pipe. She asked her daughter – but her daughter was having a rest and was too lazy to get up. Then she asked her son, Kevin. 'O.K., Mum', he said. 'Let's go and have a look at the aerial first.' They went outside with the dog and looked up at the roof. 'Look, Mum,' said Kevin, 'All I need to do is straighten the aerial. Wait a minute.' He brought a ladder and climbed up on it, not noticing that his dog was climbing after him. Up on the roof he carefully straightened the aerial. Back down in the house they tried out the television again – and found that it was still showing only wavy lines. 'My goodness', said Mum, 'What's the matter now?' 'I don't know,' said Kevin. 'By the way, where's the dog?' The dog, of course, was still sitting up on the aerial; that was what was causing the interference.

Similar exercises can be done using odd pictures cut out of colour magazines. A number of such pictures are stuck up on the board, and the teacher improvises a story (as fantastic and improbable as she likes) that somehow brings them all in. She can help students by indicating which picture she is referring to as she goes on, or she can leave them to work out the sequence for themselves. The same activity done the other way round (with the students telling the story) is of course an excellent oral fluency exercise.

Almost inevitably, some information will be given in the listening text which could not have been known only from the pictures. In the above examples this has been kept to a minimum; but the teacher can use the pictures only as cues, and improvise very much longer passages that give a great deal of extra detail. For this, of course, she will need to prepare more, and make herself some written notes on the information she is going to add. The pictures shown in Fig. 3, for example, could be used as background to the following (intermediate level):

A: Bob, do you know who I saw the other day? Old Jake, looking terribly depressed. Did he get pensioned off at last?

B: Yes. They made him stop work after fifty years at sea. He's pretty upset about it, but what can you do? He really is past it.

A: He's all alone, isn't he?

B: Yes. His wife's been dead for years. They had one daughter, Doris, but she went off to town as soon as she left school, and he hasn't heard from her since. I hear she's making good money as a model.

A: Maybe someone could get in touch with her, get her to come back for a bit to help?

B: I don't suppose she'd come, she never got on with her father. He's a bit of a tough character, and she's as selfish as they come. Oh, I expect old Jake'll get by. He's healthy at least, comes into the clinic for a check regularly.

A: Are you his doctor?

B: No, my partner, Dr Thomas.

A: That bad-tempered old thing?

B: Oh, he isn't really bad-tempered, he just looks it. He's an excellent doctor, taught me a lot. And he has a very nice family – his wife invites me over there to supper every week, very pleasant.

A: Yes, I teach the daughter, Pam, at school. She's a bit careless and lazy about her school work – but a bright little thing and very popular with her age-group.

Apart from the pictures given in this book, there is a great deal of published material which can be used for exercises like these. Posters published specifically for English-teaching purposes, such as *Wall pictures for beginners of English* by Brian Abbs and Ingrid Freebairn and *Wall pictures for language practice* by Donn Byrne and Douglas Hall are particularly good. Books of pictures such as *What do you think?* and *Say what you think* by Donn Byrne and Andrew Wright, or *The mind's eye* by Alan Maley, Alan Duff and Françoise Grellet can also be very helpful. Picture stories for language practice can be found in L. A. Hill's

Picture composition book and in Donn Byrne's *Progressive picture compositions*. The book *The Goodbodys* by Paul Groves, Nigel Grimshaw and Roy Schofield is a good source of strip cartoons, as is your local newspaper. Finally, the textbook being used in your class may well supply some perfectly suitable visual material, which will save you looking any further.

DIAGRAMS

Maps, plans, grids, family trees and so on can be used in the same way as pictures: their content described and the students asked to link the spoken description with what they see. With diagrammatic material, however, the activity is slightly more challenging, more suitable for older students: a picture is a relatively primitive way of conveying information and readily understood, whereas a diagram is symbolic, and more difficult to interpret. For this reason the discourse accompanying such material takes on a rather more authentic flavour: diagrams are often in fact accompanied by comment and explanation. In the following examples it will be seen that the listening texts slip very naturally into the context of some kind of real-life situation.

Following a route on a map is a good example of this. Here is someone describing a tour of an island (Fig. 5). It might be appropriate to use a recording here, as it appears the traveller is speaking into a tape recorder at a point near the end of his journey, perhaps in preparation for a radio programme. The level is intermediate:

When we came to the island, we landed at the town and stayed the night with some friends. In the morning we set off round the southern coast by boat and sailed on until we came to the mouth of a river. We sailed up it a little way, but had to leave our boat behind after a few miles, as the river became too shallow. After two days' climbing we reached a lake in the mountains – what a beautiful place. But freezing cold! After one night there we were glad to leave the mountains and walk down to the desert. In a day or two we came to a huge area of sand and rocks, with no water anywhere to be seen. Luckily we later found a well where we could camp and fill our water-bottles. We went on northwards until we came to the sea and then turned west along the beach. After a while we found our way blocked by a marsh. We could find no way across it at all, but there was an old boat on the beach in which we were able to sail round the coast as far as the mouth of another river. We went up it a little way and soon found ourselves in the middle of a thick forest. Using our compass, we made our way due south until we saw ahead of us on the hill a ruined castle. We are now sitting at the top of one of the towers. What a wonderful view!

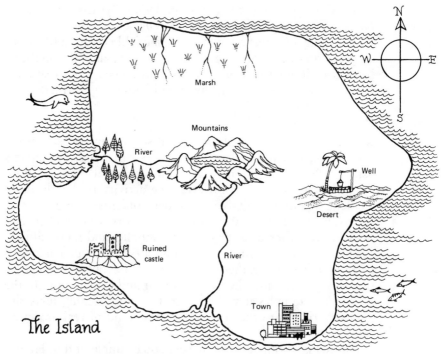

Fig. 5

Following a route according to a road map is a totally different business, and tends to lend itself to the use of different language functions – giving instructions in particular. Here is a housewife giving a girl some errands to do in town (Fig. 6); the girl is new to the area and does not yet know her way around. The speaker's home is marked E. The level is similar to that of the previous exercise.

There's not many things to do, Jessie, but you'd better take this map so that you don't get lost, and you can mark on it where you have to go. When you come out of the house, turn left and go down to the junction. Turn right, go past the swimming-pool and you'll come to Main Street. There you turn left and go along the street, over the bridge. On the other side of the bridge there's a crossroads; if you go straight across it you'll find the shopping centre on your left. Go in there and buy the things on my list. When you come out again, look for Turton Road, and go along it to the end. You'll see a football ground ahead of you. Go in there and buy two tickets for the match this afternoon. From the football ground, turn left towards the river, and go on until you come to Riverside Road. There you turn left and then immediately right again over the bridge. On the other side of the bridge you'll find a park on your right and then a little further along there's a cinema on a corner to your left. Please go in there and get their programme of forthcoming films. Then you can come home along School Road – go all the way along it until you get to Main Street again, which you cross, and you'll find a little path behind the swimming-pool; it's a short cut home.

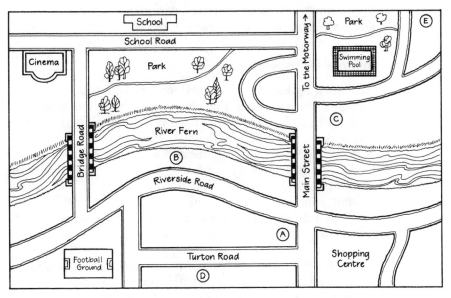

Fig. 6

Route-description is very easy to improvise; any kind of map can be used, and the teacher can lightly sketch in on her copy a line showing where her route will lead. She then describes where to go, adding comments on the scenery, or reasons for visiting particular places as she goes. The examples given here are based on imaginary places; but of course if maps of the school area, or of places in English-speaking countries which the teacher really has visited, are used, then this is all to the good: the content is 'real' and correspondingly more interesting.

Grids, graphs, plans, family trees and so on can be used the same way: the filled-in diagrams shown in Figs. 25c, 26c, 30 and 31a for example can be presented and commented on by the teacher, or accompanied by listening texts like those suggested on pp. 108–10, 116, 122–3 and 125–6 respectively.

Diagrammatic large-format material for this sort of activity can, in a school, often be borrowed from other members of staff: maps from the geography teacher, graphs and sketches from the science teachers. But authentic material of this kind may sometimes include too much difficult written English for many of our students. Listening comprehension books are increasingly using diagrams, and some good illustrations may be found in *Are you listening?* by Wendy Scott and *Task Listening* by Lesley Blundell and Jackie Stokes. Finally, the two books by Shiona Harkess and John Eastwood, *Cue for a drill* and *Cue for communication* are full of authentic-seeming but not too difficult types of diagrammatically presented information that are ideal for use in listening exercises like those suggested here.

Informal teacher-talk

According to one very influential modern school of educational thought, teachers tend to talk too much in the classroom: students learn by speaking and acting themselves, and therefore the more they do this, and the more the teacher keeps quiet, the better. This is valid up to a point; but the fact remains that the teacher possesses the information, skills or whatever that the students want, and unless she herself imparts them, the students are not going to learn very much. This is particularly true of language teaching, since language is an arbitrary set of symbols and cannot possibly be learnt by discovery or imaginative conjecture on the part of the learners: the model must be supplied by the teacher. And yet many of us have to struggle with an uneasy feeling that we are too voluble, that we really ought to confine our own talking to the absolute minimum.

Of course it is important for students to have time to practise the language skills on their own. But it is no less important for them to have plenty of opportunity of listening to good speakers of English – of whom the most conveniently available one is their teacher. Informal teacher-chat is excellent listening material, arguably the best there is. It can be interpolated at any stage in the lesson, serving as a relaxing break from more intensive work. It is easy to listen to, since it is 'live' and *personal* – intended specifically for the ears of these particular students by this particular teacher here and now – and often touches on topical subjects. Here are some suggestions for topics:

– a member of your family
– a friend / someone you have met
– something you like doing
– a place you know or have known
– your childhood
– a happy/unhappy/frightening/amusing/surprising experience
– something you did that you are proud or ashamed of
– a film or play you have seen / a book or article you have read
– your favourite hobby/food/clothes

– your plans for the future: holiday/weekend/tomorrow . . .
– your opinions on topical or local issues

Many of these – particularly the last – may lead naturally to talk by students on similar subjects.

Entertainment

If students are listening to something entertaining, then they are likely to attend and get full benefit from the listening experience. Moreover, the occasional introduction of pleasurable components like songs and stories into English lessons can improve student motivation and general morale, and show the language in a new light – not just as a subject of study, but as a source of enjoyment and recreation. Such activities are restful too: so that they provide useful interludes to put in before or after more demanding exercises, or at times when student concentration is at a low ebb (last lesson on a Friday, for example!).

STORIES

Stories, if interesting and well-told, are readily listened to by most people, and are particularly popular with younger learners. In most textbooks there are stories or anecdotes of one kind or another, used as intensive reading: as a basis for comprehension questions, for teaching vocabulary or grammar, for literary analysis or whatever. And there are hundreds of readers for learners of English as a foreign language, mostly composed of stories simplified to the various levels. Stories there are, in short, to suit every taste and every level of proficiency. But I suggest here that we use them neither for intensive language-learning nor for extensive reading, but simply let students listen to them for fun.

Some stories, if they are short, can be retold by the teacher in class in her own words, probably the most natural story-telling situation, and the one that is most warmly responded to by hearers. Suitable stories for informal narration, and some excellent ideas on their presentation and follow-up can be found in *Once upon a time* by John Morgan and Mario Rinvolucri.

But sometimes such spontaneous retelling is not practical: the story is too long or too complex, or the teacher finds story-telling too much of a burden. Then the answer is to read the story aloud, in which case we forgo some spontaneity and immediacy of communication between narrator and listeners, but we gain on other counts: the story may be more carefully constructed and better expressed, the teacher has an easier job, and the narrative may be more fluent and longer. Spontaneity and immediacy of communication may be preserved to an extent if the teacher reads well: if she looks at the text only the minimum amount needed to absorb the words, and otherwise directs her eyes and attention to the class; if she puts plenty of vocal and facial expression into her reading; and if she is constantly conscious of the probable response of her students, altering, adding and omitting bits to suit their level of understanding, sense of humour, and so on.

Stories recorded on tape as straight narrative are on the whole less easily listened to than those told or read by the teacher. Students need to concentrate far harder in order to understand them and some of the enjoyment is lost. However, if the recordings are done as dramatized versions of the stories, using different voices and background effects, then they can be exciting to listen to; and they may be further enhanced by the use of accompanying pictures or slides, in which case we are getting nearer to the kind of entertainment provided by films or television programmes (see pp. 66–7).

For reading aloud, I prefer long stories or entire books told in instalments, for two reasons. First, it takes an effort for the students to absorb a new situation or set of characters each time, and these are not always interesting; whereas with a fairly exciting serial they know what it is about and are motivated to find out what happens next, particularly if the teacher manages to stop at an exciting point each time. Second, most 'short' stories are not short enough to read in five or ten minutes – and I do not think that it is efficient use of time to take more than that, usually, for this kind of listening activity; whereas an episode in a serial can be as long or as short as the teacher likes to make it. Stories for this purpose should be chosen for the interest of their plot rather than for their literary value.

The best source for stories to read aloud is the material published by companies such as Longman, Heinemann, Macmillan and others in the form of slim booklets designed for individual extensive reading: Longman's Structural Readers are a good example. Most of these are based on fiction – simplified adaptations of classics or best-sellers, or specially written – and cover such a wide range of levels and interests that something can be found to suit every class. Some are published also as cassette recordings, often attractively dramatized.

SONGS

Songs are taught for a variety of purposes: for the sake of the vocabulary or structures they contain; to get students to produce oral English by singing them; as an aspect of English-language culture; for fun. With the first two of these objectives, songs are used mainly for the sake of the language they contain, whereas with the second two they are taught as sources of pleasure in their own right. For the first, specially-composed English-teaching songs are frequently used; for the second, 'authentic' ones. Naturally in teaching the two aspects are mixed to some extent: one hopes students will enjoy language-teaching songs, and that they will learn something from the language of authentic ones; but the distinction is, I think, a valid one.

Personally I prefer to teach authentic songs for the sake of their pleasure-giving and cultural value, treating the language aspect as an ancillary bonus. This is partly because in my experience the linguistic material contained in songs transfers badly. That is to say, students do not seem very easily to take over grammatical patterns or words they have learnt through songs into their normal spoken or written discourse, whereas similar material learnt in spoken dialogue is comparatively readily adopted. I think this is because of the interference of the melody: the phrases are so strongly connected with their tune that it is not easy to 'transpose' them into normal speech. Be that as it may, and for whatever reason they are taught, authentic well-known songs have one big advantage over 'fabricated' ones, and that is that they are (usually) simply better compositions: they give more pleasure to listen to and they can stand being heard many times. For this reason they are most suitable as a basis for pleasurable listening.

There are two periods of pleasurable listening in a typical song-learning process in the foreign-language classroom: the beginning, when students hear the song for the first time and try to catch as many of the lyrics as they can; and the end, when they know the song well, and can appreciate it and enjoy it to the full. In between there is a time when listening is less important, during which students are using the written text to help them understand the sung words, and the teacher is explaining or discussing with the class linguistic or cultural aspects of the song that she wishes to bring out. On the whole we get more pleasure from songs we are familiar with, whose words and tune we know, than from those we hear for the first time. A good song, therefore, should not be discarded once it has been taught, but can be heard at intervals again and again; students will continue to listen to, understand and enjoy it.

The choice of songs will depend partly on what is available – what the teacher or school has ready recorded or can easily acquire. Obviously, the linguistic content of the song should not be too difficult, and the words should be distinctly heard; given these two conditions, the choice of songs will be based on a compromise between the teacher's tastes and those of her students. Students are unlikely to attend well to songs they do not like – but equally, the teacher should enjoy the songs she uses, otherwise she will probably not teach them very well.

Fashions change rapidly, tastes differ, and therefore it is not easy to recommend actual songs in a book like this. However, here are a few sources of songs that have been found effective by teachers:

Folk: American and English folk or folk-style songs as sung and/or composed by: Peter, Paul and Mary; Pete Seeger; Bob Dylan; Joan Baez; Roger Whittaker; The Weavers; The Dubliners; The Spinners.

Pop: the latest hits, if clearly sung; older well-known songs such as those by: the Beatles; Simon and Garfunkel; Carole King.

Musicals: clearly sung, tuneful songs from, for example: *West Side Story; Oliver!; Fiddler on the Roof; Joseph and his Amazing Technicolor Dreamcoat; Jesus Christ Superstar; Evita; Cats; The Sound of Music,* and other Rodgers and Hammerstein shows.

For some recorded songs composed specifically for English-teaching purposes, see the *Bibliography* under *Songs*.

FILMS AND TELEVISION PROGRAMMES

Films and television or video programmes can also provide some enjoyable listening if they are based on good stories or interesting topics. There is plenty of visual reinforcement to the spoken text, and television and films are associated in the students' minds with pleasurable recreation.

However, there are various practical problems involved.

Outside the English-speaking countries most films and television programmes in English are subtitled or dubbed (unless they are specifically designed to teach English). Dubbing, of course, means that no English is heard at all; and subtitling is distracting: when you can understand the language of the subtitles it is very difficult to concentrate on the spoken English even if the latter is your native language, let alone if it is not. A selection of films or video tapes that have not been dubbed or subtitled is usually available from the British Council or from the embassies of other English-speaking countries; but their subject-matter is mostly limited to information on various aspects of these countries.

Another problem with films and television programmes designed to entertain is their length. Few good ones are short enough to provide the kind of pleasant interlude of listening within a lesson that can be provided by a story or song. If we are going to use these media, then we will usually have to take a whole lesson or double period. Obviously this cannot be done very often.

Finally there are the technical problems. Even assuming that the school has video equipment and a film projector available, all sorts of preparations have to be made. The usual classroom may not be suitable and a new room may have to be booked, the projector may have to be set up and the film inserted, the video-tape rewound to the right place, the screen put up – all this takes time. Then there are the occasional hitches: the film tears or jams, the video colour will not adjust, the sound is indistinct (this is a problem particularly with the loudspeakers of small film projectors).

I do not mean to imply by all this that films and television should not be used. On the contrary, they are an excellent medium for giving students some entertaining and useful listening practice, and series of television programmes designed to teach English are regularly and successfully used in many countries. But the use of the occasional entertaining film or television programme for 'listening for fun' should be approached with caution. The teacher should choose her material carefully, taking into account its length, level, and intrinsic interest value for the students; it is important for her to watch it herself before presenting it in class. She should not show such programmes too often; and she should be aware of the amount of technical preparation that may be necessary.

5.2 Listening and making short responses

In these exercises the listening material consists typically of long sequences of colloquial speech (monologue or dialogue) broken up into short 'bits', many of which require immediate brief responses by the learner. Thus, students are responding to each item of information as it comes up and not, on the whole, to the gist of an entire passage at once. The first seven sections of 5.2 describe short game-like activities which require either no learner-materials at all, or at the most a pencil and piece of paper. The exercises in *Pictures, Maps* and *Ground-plans* are

slightly more demanding, and are based on the use of pictures
and diagrams, copies of which are distributed to students and
then marked by them in some way in response to heard
information.

The teacher-feedback in most cases is best given quite frequently during the course of the exercise (unless the latter is very
short) in the form of a quick oral check: 'What was your
answer? . . . Good – does everyone agree? . . . anyone have
anything different? . . .'

Obeying instructions

In these exercises students are given commands, and show
comprehension by complying with them. Three main kinds of
response-activity are suggested here: physical movement, building models, and picture dictation.

PHYSICAL MOVEMENT

At the elementary level, commands may be as simple as: stand
up, sit down, go to (something), put your hand on (something),
take the (something), look at the (something), shut/open (something). Later, more advanced instructions may be used: lay your
books along the edge of your desk, fold your arms, and so on.

I have found that strings of commands like this, given briskly
and with immediate teacher-feedback, provide good practice
and are motivating in themselves. However, one or two variations can add extra motivation: the old game 'Simon says', for
example, when only the command prefixed by the words 'Simon
says' is to be obeyed, the rest ignored. In the original game
anyone who makes a mistake is 'out' and stops playing. In an
English lesson it is a pity to cut down the participation of
students in this way – particularly as those students who are
'out' first are likely to be those who most need the practice! It is
better to tell everyone to keep on participating, each one
counting how many mistakes he made, and a rough check being
made at the end to see who did well ('How many people made
less than three mistakes?').

In another variation, the teacher does an action herself which
may or may not be the same as the command she has given.
Thus students have to be on the alert, and perform what she
says, not what she does. Again, this adds motivation and makes
students concentrate on listening.

Students can also be instructed to take up a certain more or
less complex physical position involving various movements.

The teacher prepares a sketch of a certain physical attitude and instructs students how to assume it, bit by bit: 'Lie down on the floor, put your left foot on your right knee, put your finger on your nose . . .' etc. If she sees someone doing it wrong, she can of course repeat, rephrase, emphasize the key words: 'No, your *left* leg, Dan!'. See Fig. 7 for some examples of positions.

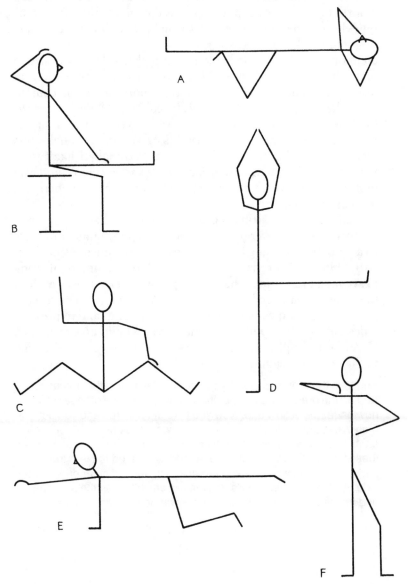

Fig. 7

CONSTRUCTING MODELS

Exercises such as the above, involving physical jerks of one kind or another, are of course more suitable for younger learners. Building a model according to specification, however, can be done by students of any age.

From what should such models be built? Plastic materials such as clay, sand or plasticine are a bit messy and rather too amorphous for our purposes; we need components that can be quickly and neatly assembled to make a well-defined shape: building-blocks or solid shapes of some kind. It is best if these components are of varied colour and perhaps shape and size to make it easier to identify them, and to allow for variety of instructions and finished product. The more varied the components the more advanced, generally speaking, will be the level of the exercise be. 'Lego' is excellent for such exercises; it is almost universally available, and tremendously versatile, though most sets are rather limited in colour range. Personally I like Cuisenaire rods even better, as they have more varied colours and also number values which can be referred to, but they are, perhaps, less easy to come by.

Preparing and distributing the components takes some time; for this reason I prefer on the whole to keep the number of these to a minimum. If using Cuisenaire rods, each student usually has two white ('one') rods, and one of each of the others; if using Lego, then each student has five eight-pin bricks, one of each of the basic colours (red, yellow, blue, black, white). The teacher prepares her own construction, or a sketch of it, and improvises a description from which students have to build an exact copy. Here, for example, is a description of the Cuisenaire rod design in Fig. 8a, for beginners:

You take the orange rod and you put it on the table – the orange rod. And on the orange rod you put the yellow, so that the orange rod is now under the yellow one. Now you take the blue rod and you put it on the yellow, and on the blue you put the two white ones, not very near each other, one at one side and one at the other side . . . and between these two white rods you put the red rod, so the red rod is in the middle, with one white rod on one side of it, and the other on the other side. And the two white rods and the red are sitting on the blue one and the blue is on the yellow, with the orange one underneath.

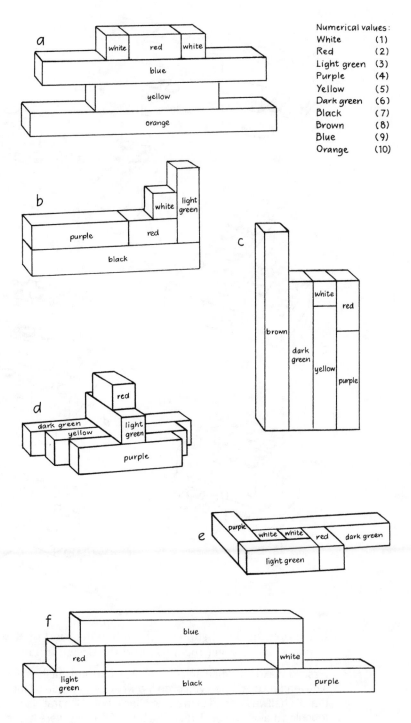

Fig. 8

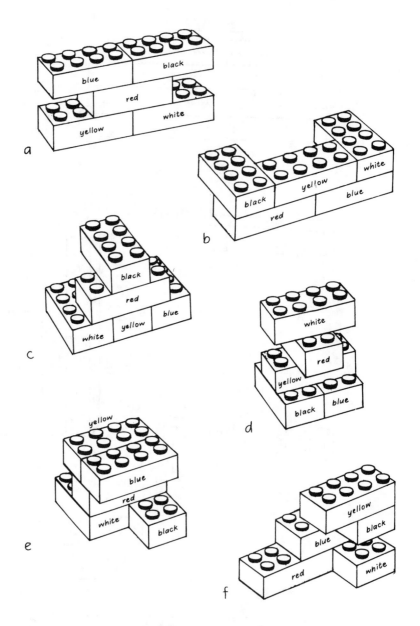

Fig. 9

For more advanced students the following kind of description might be used to get them to build the design in Fig. 9e:

First you take the white and black bricks and you put them side by side lengthways. Then you slide the white brick a little bit forward so that it's halfway ahead of the black brick, but still parallel to it, and still touching it along its back half. Got that? As if they were two feet walking, one slightly ahead of the other, but the heel of one still next to the toes of the other. Then across the parts that are still touching – that's to say, the heel and toes as it were – you put a red brick and you press it down, so it joins them together – makes a sort of bridge between them. Now on top of the red brick we're going to put the blue brick and the yellow brick. They're not going the same way as the white and black bricks, but across them, parallel to the red brick that they're going to be standing on. They're lying along the red brick so that four pins along one side of the blue brick are pressed down onto four pins along one side of the red, and four pins on one side of the yellow are pressed onto the other four pins of the red. I haven't said which side the yellow is and which the blue: well, the blue is on the side where the black brick is sticking out underneath, and the yellow is over the white.

The designs shown in Figs. 8 and 9 are all based on the limited number of components recommended above – which does not mean that they are all easy to describe or build; on the whole they get more difficult as they go on. However, if the teacher is working with small and fairly advanced classes, she can of course add to the number and variety of components and work with far more elaborate designs. The Lego company supplies plenty of well-drawn designs to go with their product, of every degree of complexity. But personally I find it more convenient to make up my own constructions on the spot, in the classroom, hidden behind a book, even if these are less elegant and completely abstract.

PICTURE DICTATION

Drawing a picture from verbal instructions is an activity that is more readily done by younger learners. This is, I suppose, because most young children enjoy drawing more than their elders do, and are less critical of the standard of their own results. However, older students may be helped by being shown how to draw stick-figures and -animals. My students derive additional encouragement from the fact that my own drawings on the blackboard are so bad; but other teachers may not have the luck to be so completely lacking in artistic talent as I am!

An improvisation based on the following description resulted in the picture shown in Fig. 10. The pupil was nine years old, in her first year of English:

There's a table in the middle of the picture and a cat is under the table. He's a white cat. Near the table is a chair. There's a very fat boy sitting on it. He's very fat indeed, and very happy, because there's a big cake on the table and he's going to eat it in a minute. The cat is happy too; he's going to eat the mouse which is under the fat boy's chair.

Fig. 10

Even easier picture dictations of this type can be based on simple items dictated as a series: 1 a chair, 2 a boy, 3 a house, and so on. Numbers, colours and shapes may also be used.

The kind of description quoted above is very easy to improvise and suitable for beginner learners. For more advanced ones, however, the teacher may find it helpful to take a real picture (from a book or cut out of a magazine), and try to get her students to reproduce it from her description. The results are entertaining in themselves, and fun to compare with the original. As with many of these exercises, the same activity done by the students themselves, in pairs, gives excellent oral fluency practice.

Ticking off items

This exercise is usually based on a list of words which the learner listens to and ticks off or categorizes as he hears them. The most well-known form of this is 'Bingo' (or 'Lotto'). Here, each student has a board with some pictures, words or numbers on it which he covers as he hears them called out. The first to cover all his items wins. This is a good and popular game, particularly with younger pupils. The only problem is the buying or making up of the boards and little item-cards that go with them; ready-made games seldom cover exactly the range of items you would like to have, and home-made ones take a long time to make. One neat way to solve this problem has been suggested by Andrew Wright in *Teaching children*. A number of items – say ten – is displayed on the blackboard or using the overhead projector. These items may be words, numbers or very simple sketches. Each student is asked to select any four of them to copy onto a piece of paper. The teacher then calls out the names of the items in random order, and the students tick them off as they hear them. This, I have found, is an excellent way of familiarizing students with newly learnt words, as well as giving listening practice. One other improvement I would suggest is to have the *last* student to mark off all items be the winner instead of the first; that way all the items are called out, and the practice is more thorough.

Students can be asked to divide the items into classes or categories instead of identifying each one separately. For this they have before them two or three empty columns with headings such as: furniture/clothes; animals/birds; red things / blue things / yellow things; round things / not-round things; food/drink; things you can eat / things you can't eat; and so on. The students can prepare these columns themselves, with headings, in a minute or two. They then hear, from the teacher or from a recording, a list of items, and for each item they identify they put a tick in the right column. The following easy list for example:

chair, table, dress, jeans, television, shoe, coat, shirt, bed, hat

would result in something like this:

Clothes   *Furniture*

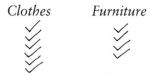

In slightly more advanced form, the items can be embedded in a coherent passage of discourse:

Good morning, I'd like a cup of coffee please, and a small piece of cake. My husband will have a cup of tea with some biscuits and cheese. And could you bring a glass of milk for my little girl, with a slice of bread and butter? And if it isn't too much trouble – a bowl of water for the dog.

but the resulting student-response is the same type as the above:

Food   *Drink*

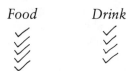

Teacher-feedback consists simply of checking that the students have the right number of ticks in each column. However, if they made a lot of mistakes or found the exercise difficult, the teacher may need to go through it again slowly, ticking off the items on the blackboard as they come up, before trying another example. It might seem that students would be able to make some wrong answers and still get the right number of ticks in each column – they could, for example, tick 'coat' as furniture and 'table' as clothes. However this in practice happens only very rarely, normally wrong answers produce the wrong number of ticks.

Again, exercises like this can be improvised using vocabulary recently learnt in class. They are particularly suitable for the elementary stages when vocabulary tends to be taught round topics: the house, clothes, animals, the body, colours, professions and so on. Similar exercises can, however, be constructed using much more advanced lexis.

The preparation of such exercises is quick and easy. The teacher prepares her headings, and writes in the appropriate columns the items she is going to mention. She may also note the number in each column, to save counting later, and a suggested context. She then either calls the items out in random order, or makes up a monologue which would naturally include them, using her suggested context as a basis. The preparatory note for the second exercise given above might look like this:

Food	*Drink*
cake	tea
cheese	coffee
biscuits	milk
bread	water
butter	
5	4

(ordering food in a restaurant)

Here are some more suggestions:

1 *Colours*	*Clothing*		2 *Wood*	*Metal*
red	dress		chair	clock
yellow	bag		table	scissors
green	shoes		pencil	radio
black	bag		shelf	
blue	coat		door	
white				
7	5		5	3

(describing what a woman is wearing) (describing classroom)

3 *Round things*	*Rectangular things*	4 *Soft things*	*Hard things*
oranges	packet of	cotton wool	apples
apples	margarine	white cheese	potatoes
eggs	book	blanket	pencils
football	pencil-box	margarine	cups
	ruler	hand-cream	plates
	radio		
	cassette		
4	6	5	5
(shopping list)		(shopping list)	

5 *Movement*	*Speech*	6 *Live things*	*Lifeless things*
went	talked	tree	mountain
sat down	said	pony	rock
got up	laughed	grass	lake
went away	called	bushes	cave
jumped	shouted	sheep	hill
ran	answered	birds	
6	6	6	5
(walking with a friend)		(landscape)	

7 *Good qualities*	*Bad qualities*
attractive	overweight
nice smile	conceited
intelligent	wasteful
kind	lazy
rich	
5	4

(describing someone)

True/false exercises

This is a very simple and well-known family of exercises, in which the students are presented with a spoken statement and asked to say whether it is true or false. Almost any type of written or spoken discourse or visual aid can serve as a basis for them, so can known facts or stories. There are, too, plenty of ways of varying the response. The students can be asked to note down the truth/falsity value of each statement in the form of words ('yes' or 'no'), letters ('T' or 'F'), or symbols ($\checkmark$ or $\times$). They can be asked to respond with a physical action: raising different-coloured pieces of paper, or objects, or cards with 'yes' or 'no' written on them; or simpler, raising their right hands for 'true' and left for 'false'. Alternatively they can be asked to respond orally: shouting out the answer, or, more effectively, repeating the true statements and keeping silent after the false ones. Finally, they can note down the number of true and false statements in separate columns as in the previous exercise.

The statements to be judged can relate to general facts ('Elephants are green', 'We can drink water'), or to immediate present reality ('The sun is shining', 'My name is Macnamara'). Or they can be based on material recently learnt: words (' "Entrance" is the opposite of "exit" ', 'A "battle" is something you eat'), or statements about the characters or plot of a story.

Visual material is another easily-used basis for this kind of exercise. Using the picture in Fig. 2, the teacher might suggest statements like: 'There are two women on the bench', 'The boy is standing still', 'There is a pigeon on the man's shoulder'. But not all true/false statements have to be quite so simple. If a group of more advanced students use the graphs shown in Fig. 31, then statements might be something like: 'All crops increased their yield per acre between 1936 and 1951' or 'Barley showed the highest yield per acre of all crops in 1966'.

The easiest preparation for such an exercise is a brief note to represent each statement, with a cross or tick to indicate its truth value, to be expanded by the teacher into full sentences as she goes. Notes for the statements in the previous paragraph referring to the 'Park' picture might look like this:

two women $\checkmark$
boy – still $\times$
pigeon on man's shoulder $\times$

Such notes can, of course, be expanded into 'yes/no' questions instead of statements: 'Are there three women in the park?', 'Is the boy standing still?' etc.

True/false exercises, as mentioned above, are very usefully exploited to revise material learnt in the class; they can also be based on what is being learnt in other lessons – history, geography, science and so on. Obviously, I can give no examples of such specific material. But here are some sample exercises based on the pictures, maps and diagrams in this book, and on general knowledge, which the teacher might be able to use:

Listening and making short responses

1   *Based on Fig. 2*
two women ✓
boy – still ✕
pigeon on man's shoulder ✕
some trees ✓
statue of woman on horse ✕
both women – black hair ✕
birds in sky ✕
man has hat ✓
woman has hat ✕
six people in picture ✕

2   *Based on Fig. 11*
picture of woman ✓
night ✕
dog under table ✕
two chairs near table ✓
tape-recorder on shelf ✕
boy in room ✕
flowers on table ✓
telephone ✓
kitchen ✕
no books ✕

3   *Based on Fig. 5*
island ✓
uninhabited ✕
lake in mountains ✓
two rivers ✓
no water in desert ✕
castle near sea ✓
forest between mountains
  and sea ✓
two towns ✕
airfield ✕
good roads marked ✕

4   *Based on Fig. 30*
John married to Ann ✕
Ann – two children ✕
Daniel – Sam's father ✓
Tom – married to Amy ✓
Tom – Kathy's cousin ✓
Jack – Kathy's uncle ✓
Mary – Amy's mother ✕
John – Jack's mother [sic] ✕
Jack – John's son ✓
Amos – 2 wives ✓

5   *Based on Fig. 31*
all crops increased yield per acre 1936–51 ✓
all crops increased yield per acre 1951–66 ✓
all crops increased production 1936–51 ✓
all crops increased production 1951–66 ✕
barley – more than 8 m. tons in 1966 ✓
highest yield per acre in 1966 – barley ✕
lowest yield per acre in 1931 – potatoes ✓
potatoes – only about 10 cwt. per acre in 1966 ✓
oats – lowest production in 1951 of all crops shown ✕
sugar beet – in general higher yield per acre than potatoes ✓

6   *General facts (easy)*
one can drink water ✓
sun in daytime ✓
man has four legs ✕
eight days in week ✕
eat breakfast in morning ✓
orange – round ✓
grass – red ✕
fish live in water ✓
baby can read ✕
river – to sea ✓

7   *General facts (harder)*
water – a liquid ✓
New York – capital of US ✕
Picasso – Italian ✕
no air on moon ✓
gold – from mines ✓
mosquitoes carry malaria ✓
Hamlet written by Shakespeare ✓
George Washington – in
  American Civil War ✕
must have oxygen to live ✓

Occasional true/false exercises, with recorded texts, can be found in most of the books listed under *Task-centred listening* in the *Bibliography*.

Detecting mistakes

This is a type of activity that students find enjoyable. It is in fact a slightly more sophisticated version of the true/false exercises described above. However, instead of evaluating the truth of each separate statement as it is said, students listen to longer passages, responding only when they come across something wrong. This something wrong may be an erroneous detail in the narration of a well-known story; or it may be a mistake in terms of reality (an impossibility, or something the students know to be in fact otherwise); or it may just be a word or phrase that does not go with what was said before (an inconsistency or contradiction). Mistakes of grammar are not used – we are, after all, practising comprehension of meaning, not mastery of grammatical rules.

Students may react immediately to mistakes, shouting out or raising their hands; or they may volunteer corrections; or they may simply make a mark on a piece of paper for every mistake they hear and see if they get the correct number of marks. It is best to check students' results, if these are written down, after every four or five mistakes, not to wait until the end of the whole passage. If responses are oral, then of course the teacher will be able to check each one as it comes up.

Every culture has its set of popular folk-tales and fairy stories; and some European tales have become known all over the world. It is no problem to find a simple story that all the students know, and tell it, introducing mistakes as you go. The story of Goldilocks, for an elementary class, might begin like this:

Once upon a time there was a little boy called Goldilocks.
She was called Goldilocks because she had the most beautiful long green hair, like gold. One day, Goldilocks went for a walk in the forest and lost her way. Suddenly she saw a little house. The window was open so she walked in. This was really the house of the three crocodiles . . .

Another idea is to describe something the students can see, with obvious mistakes. This can be the room in which the lesson is taking place, the view from the window, or the appearance of one or more of the students themselves. It can also, of course, be a picture or other visual aid. A description of the picture in Fig. 11 could run as follows (again at a fairly elementary level):

Fig. 11

This is a nice comfortable room, with a sofa, chairs, television, rug. What a lovely little puppy under the table. And there are plates and cups on the table . . . and spoons, forks, and knives . . . and a vase with a tree in it. Behind the table on the wall there's a picture of a horse, and if you look out of the window you can see the full moon shining on the sea.

More advanced exercises can be built round descriptions or stories that include things that are impossible, or at least extremely unlikely, like the Baron Munchausen stories, or parts of Alice in Wonderland. Here is a home-made example (intermediate level):

When I got up this morning I was very hungry, so I went and made myself some breakfast. I can only eat soft food (I have no teeth), so I boiled my eggs a good long time until they had softened down enough to eat. I then made myself a pot of good strong tea and spread it thickly on a piece of buttered bread. Delicious. Finally, I washed the dishes. I use clean air for washing the dishes, that way I don't get my hands wet and there is no need to dry up afterwards . . .

Another type of passage has internal inconsistencies: that is to say, one part of it contradicts, or is inconsistent with, another. Here is such a passage, of high intermediate level:

Good morning, ladies and gentlemen. This is your captain, the pilot, speaking. Welcome aboard the Boeing 747, our biggest ship. The time is twelve midnight and we have just taken off from London on our flight to New York. We shall be flying due east. The sky here is clear, but most of the Indian Ocean, over which we shall be flying, is covered with cloud, so we shall not see much of it. The weather in New York is, I am sorry to say, rather unpleasant: there is a heatwave on, and the temperature is below zero. However, it may improve by the time we get there. In a short time I shall give you further details of our height, air-speed and estimated time of take-off. I hope you enjoy the crash. Thank you.

Finally, the teacher may take a story or information-giving text of any kind and deliver it twice, introducing deliberate but plausible mistakes the second time. In this case the students rely on their memory to detect the errors.

The best way to prepare material of this kind is again by using notes, unless the passage is fairly formal (as in the last example above), where it may be better to use a full text. Mistakes are underlined, with the correct version given immediately afterwards in brackets, and the teacher simply works them in as she goes on. The more ridiculous the mistakes are, the better: younger students like the substitution of crocodiles for bears, older ones are entertained by the idea of enjoying an aeroplane crash; and provided the teacher delivers the whole with a dead-pan face and relates seriously to the actual learning activity involved, the comic element can only add to the good humour and willingness of the class. Here are some notes for exercises of this type:

1   *Goldilocks and the three bears*
Boy (girl) with green (fair, yellow) hair . . . saw window (door) open . . . house of three crocodiles (bears) . . . saw three plates of macaroni (porridge) . . . big plate too hot, middle too hairy (cold), small one good, ate all. Chairs: big one too hard, middle too yellow (soft), small one good, sat, broke. Beds: big one too small (hard), middle too soft, small comfortable, slept. Bears came back: Father Bear: 'Who's been sitting in (eating) my porridge?' . . . Mother Bear . . . Baby Bear. Father: 'Who's been eating (sitting in) my chair?' . . . Mother Bear . . . Baby Bear. Father: 'Who's been dancing (lying) in my bed?' Baby Bear: 'Look who's in my bed! A baby hippopotamus! (little girl)' . . . ending as original.

2   *Based on Fig. 11*
Puppy (cat) . . . knives (–) on table . . . tree (flowers) in vase . . . picture of horse (woman) . . . full moon (sun) on sea (field) . . . three (two) chairs near table . . . curtains closed (open) . . . someone (no one) sitting on sofa . . . Bible on television (shelf) . . . room very untidy (tidy).

Fig. 12

3 *Based on Fig. 12*
Boat going to India (China) . . . old woman looks happy (sad) . . . her daughter waving umbrella (handkerchief) . . . husband crying (laughing, smiling) . . . boy in white (black) boots . . . waving sadly (happily) . . . dog near woman (boy) . . . fast asleep (sitting, waving) . . . near dog is chicken (bird, seagull) . . . grandma is going to America (China) on jet plane (slow boat).

4 *Weather forecast*
Today it will be very rainy in most areas, so take your sunglasses (umbrellas) with you when you go out! In London and the South East it will start sunny, but clouds will soon begin to talk (appear), and by mid-morning you can expect some heavy soup (rain). In the South West, rain will start from early morning, and will continue all year (day). Moving up to the Midlands, the story is a little brighter: rain at first, but sunny intervals are impossible (possible) later, and the afternoon should be clear and snowy (sunny). Further north – rain all day, I'm afraid, and it'll be cold and windy in most houses (areas). Finally Scotland: rain, and snow on green (high) ground. Further outlook: continuing as today, cold and fine (rainy).

Aural cloze

In the conventional cloze procedure, normally used as a test of reading comprehension, a written passage is given to the learner with words deleted at regular or irregular intervals. The learner then has to use the context to fill in the missing words. Similar techniques can be used for listening comprehension, with or without a written text.

WITH A WRITTEN TEXT

The deleted version of a written text is given to the students, and the teacher simply reads out the full version while the students fill in the gaps according to what they hear. If they have had a chance to read through the passage first and fill it in as in a normal cloze exercise, then the listening will provide them with confirmation or corrections. If, however, they do not read the material beforehand then they will probably rely on their ear rather than on deduction from context to get the right answers. But filling in everything while listening takes time, so that either the teacher must slow down delivery, or read the passage several times. However, if the blanks are sufficiently widely spaced (one every two or three lines instead of one every line as in most reading cloze tests), then the teacher may read at more or less normal speed, and the students should, if they write quickly and 'skim' to catch up (useful skills to practice in themselves!), be able to manage with only one or two hearings. Songs may be used the same way: the lyrics are written out with occasional words missing, and the students fill them in while listening to the song. Again, it is important not to have the gaps at too frequent intervals.

Another variation of this which has something in common with the *Detecting mistakes* exercises described on pp. 80–3, is based on a text with no apparent blanks in it at all. The teacher reads out her version of the text in which some of the words differ from those in the students' version. The students may respond in different ways, depending on whether the spoken text is seen as 'correct' or the written. If the spoken, then the students simply correct their own texts. If the written, then they put up their hands and correct the teacher as each discrepancy is revealed.

WITHOUT A WRITTEN TEXT

The presence of a written version takes some of the pressure off the listening: students can concentrate less with their ears, as it were, because their eyes are doing most of the work. Aural cloze exercises can, however, be done using no written text – at least, for the students – in which case they are more difficult but very much more useful as preparation for one real-life listening problem: 'noise'. If a word or two is indistinct or drowned by noise, or otherwise incomprehensible to the listener, then it is important for him to be able to reconstruct as far as possible the gist of what was missing (not necessarily the actual words). By deliberately obliterating occasional words in a listening passage we can give our students some practice in this.

Again, gaps should be far more distant from one another than those of written cloze texts, or there will not be time to cope with them. The natural way for students to respond is to call out the answers; but since these are usually short, they can also jot them down in writing as the exercise goes on. In this case, gaps should be even more infrequent, or short extracts should be used with only one gap each time, to be answered and checked before going on to the next. If students cannot think of the right English word or phrase, the native-language equivalent should also be acceptable (if, of course, the teacher understands it!). The main objective is to get at the *meaning* of the missing item(s), and if the student has guessed it, in whatever language, he has succeeded in the task. Example (intermediate level):

A: Have a good holiday, Jennie?
B: Great – the only _____ is that I don't feel like going back to work now.
A: I know, that's just how I felt last week when I came back. You'll get used to it.
B: I'm sure I will, don't have much _____, do I?
A: Sure you have a choice – you can always walk out!

In exercises like these where the gaps are only words, it is better in some ways to give nonsense words than blanks, because they supply a closer imitation of the most usual and difficult type of 'noise' for the learner: unknown vocabulary. The introduction of nonsense words causes no break in the stream of speech and can incorporate some morphological clues to meaning – prefixes, suffixes and so on – as in the following (intermediate level):

Well, as I was walking home from the pub, who should I see but my old friend Jonathan *spranking* along the street. 'Jonathan,' says I, 'you look like you've had a drop too much!' 'Me?' he says. 'Dry as a bone,' he says, 'but I just heard the most *chusterful* news! You won't believe it. Old Nell is getting married!' '*Undebigible!*' says I. 'She's ninety if she's a day!'

The teacher should, of course, make it quite clear to students that *spranking, chusterful* and *undebigible* are in fact nonexistent words in English. It may be a good idea, too, to write up the nonsense words on the board before letting students hear the passage, in order to avoid confusion with other words in the passage that they may not be familiar with – or they may be led to think that these too are nonsense! If the teacher prefers not to use nonsense words, then real words that the student is unlikely to know may be used, such as *stroll, preposterous* and *incredible* in the above example. In this case, however, the teacher should be aware that the exercise is slightly less valuable as a basis for guessing-from-context: if a student knows that the word is a 'real' one, he will tend to guess it by using its similarity to other known words or roots, without reference to its context.

Cloze tests like these can be used to revise new vocabulary if each gap is designed to be filled by a recently-learnt word, or can only be filled correctly when such a word has been previously understood.

There are no published sets of ready-made aural cloze exercises that I know of; but they are easy to prepare. For the first-mentioned exercise above, where the students prepare a written cloze test and then use the heard version to check their results – ordinary cloze tests can be used as they stand. If the students are not given time to read beforehand, then similar passages should be prepared with only one word deleted every third line or so. For the 'discrepancies' version, the teacher prepares multiple copies of a text and writes in on her own copy the different words over the lightly-crossed out words of the original, so that she will be able to read out the whole smoothly:

The Pope will give a brief ~~television~~ radio address in Italy tonight despite his bout of 'flu. The Pope has been ~~advised~~ told by doctors to miss an Easter procession in which he was to have carried a wooden cross in commemoration of Christ's walk to the Crucifixion. Instead he'll speak to the ~~nation~~ people on television from his private apartment.

The Pope will also miss a midnight service tomorrow, but is expected to take part in the main Easter ~~Sunday~~ Monday Mass.

(Adapted from *Listen, then* by Paulette Møller and Audrey Bolliger)

Exercises where students cannot see the text are difficult to improvise 'live' because we have to be able to reconstruct exactly the context of each missing word for checking purposes. So either we must read aloud from a written text, or use recordings. If nonsense words are going to be substituted, then these can be written into the teacher's text as in the 'discrepancies' example above; again, the teacher can then work in the nonsense words smoothly, and easily identify their context and what they represent when the time comes to check.

Then there are the breakfast cereals. They are mostly sold in large
~~packets~~ *boogles* and eaten cold with sugar and milk. Weetabix is a breakfast
cereal which is very ~~popular~~ *peasant* in England. You'll find shredded wheat
and cornflakes on many breakfast tables too. Lately the Swiss food
called muesli has ~~become~~ *pridden* quite popular.

(Adapted from *Let's listen*, by John McClintock and Börje Stern)

If, however, the teacher prefers to leave actual blanks, then the words to be omitted can simply be lightly crossed out in the text. But in this case, the question is, how such blanks can be indicated orally. We can just leave a pause, with perhaps a gesture to show that it represents something missing. A resourceful teacher might bring a buzzer or bell of some sort into the classroom and sound it for each gap. But probably the easiest word-substitute is simply an indistinct low mumble – which is more or less the way incomprehensible words are often heard by foreigners anyway! If a recording is used, then we can simply turn down the volume at the words we wish to delete.

Almost any spoken or read material of appropriate level can be adapted for use in aural cloze exercises. Monologue is on the whole more suitable than dialogue.

Guessing definitions

This is really a guessing-game in reverse. The teacher defines or describes something (having told students in advance what nature of a thing it is), and they simply have to guess what it is – raising their hands to volunteer the answer, or jotting it down on a piece of paper.

Sometimes the things to be guessed can be one of a closed set, as for example when students have a set of pictures before them like those in Figs. 1, 3, 13, and have to identify which corresponds with the heard description. A set like Fig. 3 is, perhaps, not so good for this kind of game, because the choice is too small and the differences too obvious – any description will be very easily guessed and provide little challenge for any but the most elementary classes. Better is a set of pictures like the cartoon-strip in Fig. 13, where students really have to listen carefully to identify which picture is meant. Exactly which

McLACHLAN   Fig. 13

becomes clear in this example only with the last sentence (elementary level):

There's a man in the picture. He's wearing a coat, and he has glasses and a moustache. He is walking along in front of a wall. He doesn't look very happy. He is alone. He has a hand on his head.

A cartoon like this can be used several times, identifying a different picture each time. Similarly, portraits cut out of magazines and stuck on the blackboard can be used, or pictures of rooms or landscapes or anything else: the main point is that the different pictures should be similar enough for the students to have to listen carefully to all the information in order to choose the right answer. Some examples of suitable material are shown in Figs. 13, 14, 15.

Fig. 14

Fig. 15

Apart from visuals, anything normally used as the subject of a guessing-game can also be used for this activity: objects, people, professions, animals, places, events. The teacher jots down a list of the answers, and then improvises the descriptions. Each description is fairly short, so that ten or more such items can be given straight off in two or three minutes.

More abstract nouns, adjectives and verbs can also be used as the subjects of this exercise. It is a little more difficult to describe them than to describe objects or people, but their use does widen the range of language employed. A straight enumeration of defining characteristics can often be given ('a geometrical figure with three sides'), but not always (what are the defining characteristics of 'red'?). There are many other methods of definition available: here are some of the main ones. We can use antonyms ('It's the opposite of "deep" '), or synonyms ('It's the same as "basic" '). There are various kinds of comparison ('It's not as dark as black or as light as white, somewhere in between', or 'It's like rope, but not so thick or strong'). Examples can be given as sentences ('It's the colour of roses, or of blood') or, if the word is a class-word, as lists ('dog, mouse, dolphin, lion, monkey, but not beetle, snake, bird, fish'). A useful gimmick, particularly when the item is a verb, is 'coffee-pot', where sentences can be made up about the unknown item, substituting the word 'coffee-pot' for its name ('If you boil water, the water will coffee-pot into steam . . . benzine coffee-pots very quickly').

Such activities can usefully serve to practise or revise vocabulary the students have been recently taught.

Noting specific information

In these exercises the student is asked to listen to a passage and note down specific information from it: he therefore has to ignore some parts of it and concentrate on others. This reproduces a common real-life situation where we are 'listening out' for what we want to know and relate to the rest of what we hear as 'redundant'.

We may start by asking students to extract only one or two given items of information. They are told in advance what items to look for and have, as it were, to 'scan' the heard passage in order to pick out what they need to know. From this we progress to tasks where they have to pick up a certain type or area of information and ignore the rest, without knowing in advance how many actual items of such information will occur.

SPECIFIC ITEMS

In these exercises the ratio of insignificant to significant information is very high. Students may listen for two or three minutes in order to pick out an item lasting two seconds. They know in advance exactly what they are listening for, in the sense that they have, more often than not, a certain key word or phrase to look out for, so that when they hear it they know it will be accompanied by the information they want. They know as well exactly how much information they need; as soon as they have got it, they can 'switch off'. Supposing we give a list of football results as broadcast on the BBC – something like the following:

Here are the football results. League division I:

Aston Villa	2	Swansea	nil
Brighton	1	Birmingham	nil
Coventry	4	Everton	2

Liverpool	5	Southampton	nil
Manchester United	nil	Arsenal	nil
Norwich	1	West Bromwich	3
Notts. County	nil	Ipswich	6
Stoke	4	Luton	4
Tottenham	4	Nottingham Forest	1
Watford	8	Sunderland	nil
West Ham	4	Manchester City	1

Before listening, the students are issued a task question such as 'Did West Ham win?' or 'Who did Manchester United play?'

Broadcast flight schedules can be used similarly. The information here is slightly more involved and is given in the form of full sentences rather than in straight lists. Students might be asked: 'What is the number of the flight to New York?' or 'Is the Geneva plane taking off or landing?' or 'Which gate do I have to go to if I am flying to Madrid?' (intermediate level):

Now landing on Runway Five is Flight SK 143 from Oslo. The next flight due in at 21.30 hours is Flight BA 501 from Geneva and Paris. Will all passengers to New York on Flight TW 304 please go to Gate number six.
This is the final call for passengers to Madrid on Flight BA 692. Please go immediately to Gate twelve.

Back with the BBC, news broadcasts are an excellent base for this type of exercise. We might ask students to listen to one topic and pick out particular details. Take this for example (advanced level):

Airports are reporting heavy business as thousands of people set off on their Easter holidays. A number of airlines say there's been a big last-minute rush and British Airways are expecting record bookings with more than twenty thousand passengers flying to the Continent today. But holiday-makers may not find the sun they're seeking. Reports from European resorts are not encouraging. In most places the temperature is only in the middle fifties. Even so, that's better than in Britain. The forecasters here say it's going to be cold and windy today, with wintry showers at times. But there will be some sunny intervals.

(From *Listen, then* by Paulette Møller and Audrey Bolliger)

The question could have been: 'What's the weather going to be like in Britain?', 'What's the weather like on the Continent?', 'How many people will fly to the Continent today?' or 'What time of year is it?'

For a longer exercise an entire news broadcast could be used, and the students asked about only one of the items: 'Who won the elections?', 'Where was the Queen today?' and so on.

Conversations and monologues can also be used, students being asked simply to note only one or two of the items of information given. For the following extract, they could be asked how tall Peter Ustinov is, how long he was a soldier for, whether he is married, how many children he has:

My name is Peter Ustinov . . . I'm fifty-seven years old. I'm what is known in the American clothing trade as 'portly'. I am just under six foot tall, although if I hold myself properly I can still just about reach it. I served in the British army for four and a half years as a private, hated it and wouldn't have missed it for the world. I managed to do quite well in the theatre and the movies, being the holder of two 'Oscars'. There are only eight actors that have got more than one, so I'm very lucky in that respect. I've got four children. I've been married three times. Apart from that I really don't know what to say about myself . . .

(From *Meeting people* by Terry L. Fredrickson)

To make the activity a little more varied, different students can be asked to look out for different things, pooling their information at the end. In any case, they do not need to write down their answers in these exercises; a mental note should be sufficient, since teacher-feedback is usually given on the spot.

AREAS OF INFORMATION

Asking students to note down or remember all the items relevant to a particular area of inquiry is a more difficult and diffuse task; but it still requires as its basis that learners distinguish between essential and non-essential information. In this case there is rarely a 'key word' to trigger the hearers' response; the topic to be listened out for may be expressed in many different ways. A relatively higher proportion of the discourse will include 'essential' information; and the student must listen to the end to make sure he has gathered all relevant details. Finally, he will usually need to write down his answers, as there will be several of them, often in the shape of a list.

For instance, we might take the football results shown on pp. 91–2 and ask students to note down the number of draws; or the flight schedules, and ask which countries (not cities) were mentioned. These are fairly easy, as the separate sentences or sense-units are clearly divided from one another. But discourse that is less structured – like most spontaneous monologue or dialogue – provides more of a challenge for the student in picking out significant information and discarding the rest, and gives more useful practice.

In the following example, students could be asked to try to

reconstruct the shopping list that is the topic of conversation (intermediate to advanced level):

M: Right. Now, what have I got? Er, some cream here.
W: O.K. Fine.
M: I could only get single but you didn't actually specify on the list, I think, what you wanted.
W: Ooh dear! Well I, well I suppose yes I can beat it up with some sugar and egg yolk or something and make it thicker. What else have you got here now?
M: Strawberries I've got.
W: Yeah.
M: But just a few because they were a bit expensive.
W: How much were they?
M: These?
W: Yeah.
M: Mmm. Would you believe 40?
W: Well, all right. O.K.
M: Here you go. Now, ah, pièce de résistance. Here we are – chicken. It's quite a big one.
W: O.K.
M: Four pounds eight ounces. That do?
W: Hmm. Well, I suppose if it was the best you could get, it was the best you could get. What else have you got? Did you get the tomatoes?
M: Yes. They're somewhere down here . . .

(From *Learning to listen* by Alan Maley and Sandra Moulding)

Here is another variation: an old age pensioner is discussing the rising prices with an interviewer, and students are asked to note down which commodities have gone up in price and which down (intermediate to advanced level):

Paulette: And do you find it hard to make your housekeeping money go round?
Elizabeth: I can't make my housekeeping money go round. I'm losing ground all the time because the prices go up and up and up. It's beyond reason. Every time you go something has gone up. They don't put it up one or two pennies, they put it up about four or five pennies at a time.
Paulette: Mmm. What do you think has gone up most lately?
Elizabeth: Well, of course, our staple diet . . . we used to always have one good meat meal a day. Well, meat is an absolute luxury now.
Paulette: Mmm. What about fish?
Elizabeth: Fish is just as dear or perhaps even dearer than meat. And we have to buy . . . sausages and eggs . . . eggs are a little bit cheaper because of the time of the year, but bacon

is very dear, and we're buying lots of Danish bacon, we're buying more Danish bacon than English bacon.

Paulette: Is Danish bacon cheaper than English bacon?

Elizabeth: No, I don't think it's cheaper . . . I think it's a little bit dearer, but I think people like it more. I think they like it very much more than the English bacon. There was a great outcry about that . . . the Danish bacon market is . . . doing better than the English bacon market.

Paulette: What about things like butter . . . cheese?

Elizabeth: Cheese is very dear indeed. Butter has come down a little, tea has come down a little, coffee of course, we haven't . . . most of us haven't been able to afford to buy pure coffee for a very long time, we have to buy this instant coffee which doesn't agree with most of us because it's full of caffeine. I used to buy the caffeine-free coffee, but I can't even buy ordinary coffee now, it's so expensive.

(From *Listen, then* by Paulette Møller and Audrey Bolliger)

For single-item exercises as in *Specific items* above, any text can be used, recorded, read or improvised: all the teacher has to do is make up the question(s).

For both single-item and information-area exercises BBC reports on the news or other specific topics are particularly suitable: sports reports, financial reports, the weather, conditions in fishing areas, fashion, forthcoming programmes and so on. Each passage can be used two or three times with a different task question each time.

Some excellent listening passages giving information, which can easily be exploited for this type of exercise can be found in *Task listening* by Lesley Blundell and Jackie Stokes, and in *Learning to listen* by Alan Maley and Sandra Moulding. Similar material for beginners or younger learners can be taken from *Are you listening?* by Wendy Scott.

If the teacher wishes to improvise her own material then she makes up the list (or item) that she will want the students to note, and improvises a monologue round it. Here are some suggested topics and lists:

Packing to go away on holiday: clothes, swimming things, sunglasses, sun-cream, something to read, aspirin, first aid, paper hankies.

Shopping list: milk, margarine, bread, jam, apples, cheese, biscuits, cotton-wool, toothpaste, newspaper.

Places to visit on European tour: Paris, Nice, Rome, Florence, Venice, Geneva, Vienna, Salzburg.

Things to do today: dentist, library, buy food, wash hair, ironing, cook supper, telephone Mother, mend puncture.

Things I like doing: reading, theatre, music, meeting people, eating
out, walking, travelling.

Pictures

IDENTIFYING AND ORDERING

For this students use a series of pictures, or one picture that is
composed of several clearly differentiated components (a number of people for example). They are then asked to identify the
pictures or components as they are referred to, either naming or
numbering them in the order in which they were mentioned. The
people depicted in Figs. 1 and 3, for example, could be identified
by name using passages like those suggested on pp. 49–50 and 55
respectively. But we can only ask students to name things that
are namable (people, possibly animals and places) – whereas any
series of pictures can be numbered; so that ordering by number
is the more flexible and versatile of the two possibilities. For this,
care should be taken to use component pictures which could be
combined in more than one order – otherwise students will be
able to do the task without listening; and preferably not more
than five or six pictures should be used, or it will take too long to
scan them, particularly at the beginning of the exercise, in order
to decide which comes first. The strip shown in Fig. 16 could be
combined with one of the following passages (intermediate to
advanced level):

Well, this was lovely unspoilt country once – fields, woods, hills –
before the advent of man. Then some people came along and
decided to settle here – built a small village, and it stayed like that for
years, until there was this population explosion in the country,
tremendous amount of building, and the place mushroomed into a
thriving town overnight almost. Then there was the war . . . people
died or went away and the whole town fell into ruin . . . you can see
the remains over there.

or:

A long time ago there was a village here, so they say, but no one
knows who exactly inhabited it. When my great-great-grandfather
came here with the other settlers, there were only ruins, and it looked
like they had been standing here for a long time. Anyhow, my
great-great-grandfather and the others came here and built a big town
– and it stood here on this very spot until forty years ago, when the
whole area was taken over by the National Parks Organization. They
didn't want this ugly great town in the middle of their park, so they paid
the inhabitants compensation and razed the whole thing to the ground
with bulldozers. You'd never know today there was once a town here,
would you?

Fig. 16

Sketches or photographs representing different people can be presented together with recordings of the same people talking, and students be asked to match picture with voice; different communicative situations can be depicted and put with the monologue or dialogue that accompanies them; even a series of random pictures cut out from magazines and photocopied can be linked together by an imaginative teacher into a story or description or even just described one after the other with no connection, other than that of sequence, between them at all.

Exercises of this type can be found in the task-centred listening comprehension books listed in the *Bibliography*. Here are a few note-form suggestions of my own, to be used with the pictures in Figs. 17–20:

Fig. 17
Couple started quarrelling . . got really fierce . . . wife walked out . . . husband begged her to come back . . . made it up.

Fig. 17

or:
Used to be affectionate couple . . . started quarrelling . . . woman
walked out . . . husband begged her to come back . . . came back but
quarrelled even worse.

or:
Couple quarrelled . . . made up, embraced . . . quarrelled again even
worse . . . husband begged wife not to leave . . . but she left.

Fig. 18
Leopard chased gazelle . . . man shot leopard . . . leopard died . . .
gazelle went back to grazing.

or:
Leopard asleep . . . gazelle grazing . . . heard man shooting . . .
leopard woke, saw gazelle, chased and killed it.

or:
Leopards used to chase and kill gazelle so few left . . . man came,
killed leopards . . . now most leopards dead . . . gazelle feeding
peacefully.

Fig. 18

Fig. 19

X left school, went into army . . . university . . . played football for
university team . . . got married . . . had two children.

or:

X played a lot of football in school . . . went to university . . . married
. . . had children . . . decided on army career.

or:

X did four years in army, left . . . lived with girl-friend many years,
professional footballer . . . studying in spare time . . . two children . . .
finally decided to get married to girl-friend.

Fig. 19

Fig. 20

People going round world: by ship from New York to Africa . . .
crossed Sahara by camel . . . on foot to Damascus . . . across Asia by
jeep . . . back home by plane.

or:

Relative advantages and disadvantages of travelling by plane, ship,
jeep, foot, camel.

Fig. 20

ALTERING AND MARKING

Children particularly very much enjoy tampering with professionally drawn pictures: witness the moustaches, beards and hats drawn on to portraits, and the amount of filling-in, colouring and other kinds of artistic additions made by children to illustrations in their textbooks or story-books (if allowed!). Even older learners seem to enjoy such drawing as part of a listening exercise, provided the language practice involved is seen as serious and profitable.

Let us take a picture like Fig. 11 and add a spoken description that runs something like this (elementary level):

You can see the picture of a room. I'm going to tell you how to colour it. Are you ready?

Well, there are some flowers on the table. They're red, and they're standing in a black vase. Got that? The vase is black all over, and the flowers are red.

There's a cat under the table with a long tail. He's nearly all white, only his feet and ears are black.

Then there's the television. It's a colour television, but it isn't working very well, there's no picture, only lots of different colours all mixed up.

The woman in the picture on the wall is wearing a blue dress.
Can you see the telephone on the shelf next to the radio? It's a green telephone.
And then on another shelf on the wall there are some books. There's one book that says *English*, another that says *Bible*. The Bible is white, but the English book is orange . . .

The task is based only on colouring in this case, but it in fact practises a good deal more than just hearing and understanding names of colours. In order to do the exercise the student has to know all the language used to describe the room, its contents, and the spatial relations between them.

Not all students have colouring pens or pencils at their disposal for an exercise of this kind, but all have, or can get hold of, ordinary lead pencils. These are all that is necessary to make alterations to the picture shown in Fig. 21 according to the following passage (intermediate level):

There's a family sitting round the television . . . as you can see it's a large family. Can you see two little twins sitting by the dog on the floor? They've got bobble hats on . . . well, the bobbles are black not white, that is, the little woollen balls on top, they're black. Then there's a smaller baby sitting on the floor in the bottom right hand corner of the picture. He's also got a bobble hat on, just like the twins . . . a bobble hat, on his head, and the bobble is black again. He's holding a balloon . . . can you see him? The fat woman on the sofa sitting near the baby, the one who is reading a newspaper, she's got glasses on

Fig. 21

to help her to read, she's very shortsighted. Then the thin woman sitting next to her, the one with long hair, she's got sandals, only she's only wearing one of them, on the foot that's on the floor. The other foot is bare, she's warming it on the dog's back, and the sandal is on the floor behind the twins.

To present this kind of exercise, the teacher inserts the colours or other alterations into her copy of the picture and then explains them to the class, repeating and enlarging the information quite extensively as she goes on in order to give students time to fill in the necessary changes. All the drawings in this book could be used in this way, as could almost any black-and-white sketches that the teacher, students or school happen to have available and do not mind reduplicating and/or defacing.

Maps

NAMING FEATURES

Maps obviously lend themselves to having names written on them far more than pictures do. Here, for example, is the Island again (Fig. 22), which has only just been resettled, and the

Fig. 22

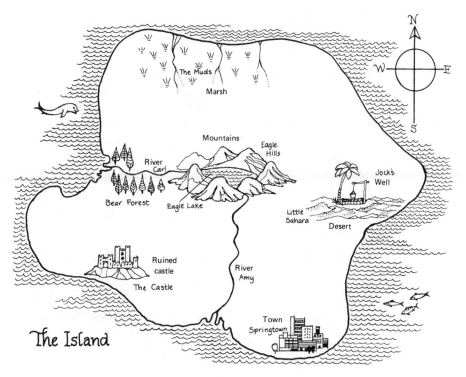

map-maker wants to know from one of the settlers how he should name the various regions and features (intermediate):

A: Well, let's start with the town where you live, Jock. What's its name?

B: We just call it 'the town' because it's the only one we've got, but I believe the founders called it Springtown because of the spring in its centre.

A: O.K., Springtown it is. Now. You have two big rivers. What are they called?

B: We called them after two of our settlers who were killed in an accident. One is River Carl, and the other is Amy.

A: Which is which?

B: River Amy is in the south, River Carl is to the west.

A: And what do you call the lake?

B: The mountains we call Eagle Hills, so the lake is Eagle Lake.

A: What about the woods to the west of the mountains?

B: That's Bear Forest – we found a family or two of bears there. To the north of the forest there is a marshy area which is known as 'The Muds'.

A: And the desert?

B: Some joker called that 'The Little Sahara', though it's very small indeed as deserts go. Then there's a small oasis with a well – it's marked on your map. That's called Jock's Well, after me. I discovered it.

A: Have you a name for the castle?

B: No, we just call it 'The Castle'. We don't know who built it. The same as those who dug the well, I suppose.

Identifying features in a town landscape seems at first sight a less interesting task, as you are limited more or less to buildings and streets, without the variety possible in a rural landscape. But one can make an interesting exercise out of a discussion like the following, where a team of town planners have five sites available (marked on Fig. 6 by the letters A to E) and have to decide where they will put a hotel, an old people's home, a multi-storey car park, a petrol station and a supermarket. The students have the different items listed under their maps; all they have to do is write the appropriate letter beside each one (slightly more advanced than the above):

Al: Right. Now I understand we have five sites available to us for the five building projects on our list.

Ben: Yes. I've marked them A, B, C, D and E on your maps. A is on the corner of Main Street and Turton Road, opposite the shopping centre, B is between the river and Riverside Road, C is beside Main Street, between the river and the swimming-pool, D is on Turton Road, at the bottom of the map, and E is at the top right-hand corner, on Park Road.

Al: Thank you, I think that is very clear. Now, we are to build a hotel, an old people's home, a multi-storey car park, a petrol station and a supermarket. Can I have any suggestions please?

Con: Well, I suggest we build the hotel at C. It's on the river, and it's very convenient for the swimming-pool and shopping centre.

Ben: I don't agree. That's a very noisy site. All the traffic coming off the motorway roars along Main Street – it's easily the busiest part of town. You want a quieter site for a hotel . . . E, or possibly B or D.

Al: I suggest B for the hotel. It's quiet without being too far from the shopping centre, and it has a nice view, we can build the rooms so that they overlook the river and park.

Ben: I agree.

Al: All right, let's go on to the petrol station. Now here we do need a site on the main road, to catch the motorway traffic. And noise doesn't matter. That means either A or C.

Con: Either would do. Let's look at the other projects. The old people's home.

Ben: Again we need somewhere quiet. D or E.

Al: E, definitely. D is far too close to the football ground. They make a lot of noise those football fans, and park their cars and motorbikes all the way down Turton Road.

Ben: Well, we can solve that problem once we've built the car park. But even so, I do agree that E is a better site. It's opposite a park too, so the old people could be taken there for walks. Now what about the car park?

Al: It might be a good idea to have it at A, convenient for shoppers in the shopping centre.

Ben: But we wanted A for the petrol station.

Con: And what about the supermarket?

Al: Hmm . . . the supermarket should be near the shopping centre, don't you think? More convenient for the shoppers. Which means it more or less has to be at A.

Ben: That solves the problem. If the supermarket is at A, then the petrol station has to be at C, that's the only other main-road site.

Al: And the car park at D. That way it'll provide facilities both for shoppers and for football fans.

ALTERATIONS

Changes can be made in maps the same way as they can be made in pictures. Let us go back to the Island (Fig. 23), listen to the head of the Island Council describing his achievements, and mark in the 'improvements' he has made (intermediate to advanced level):

Citizens of the Island! In the coming elections vote for those you can rely on, those whose achievements you can see around you. I and my

colleagues have been in office for the last ten years – ten years of
development, improvement, and a constantly rising standard of living.
The big dam to the south of the mountains for example, which
supplies hydro-electric power to the entire island – that was our first
project. Then we piped water from the lake down into the desert, so
that it is a desert no longer. There is a thriving new town where once
there was only a well, with a growing industrial area – all thanks to
constant supplies of fresh water from the mountains. Our main city to
the south has expanded along the coast, so that its western suburbs
reach almost to the river, with a corresponding rise in population. But
we have also preserved natural areas: we have fenced off the entire
mountain area and declared it a national park, and there is another
park round the ruined castle. We also had nature trails marked in the
forest – I am sure many of you have enjoyed rambling there. As to the
marsh – you remember there was once a marsh to the north? No
more. That land was drained and is now a fertile agricultural area.
Finally, you have all seen the new hotels being built to the south of
Castle Park along the coast. The beaches there are perfect for
swimming and surfing, and we hope to build up a tourist industry.

These achievements speak for themselves! Vote for us, for the
continuing development and prosperity of your Island!

Fig. 23

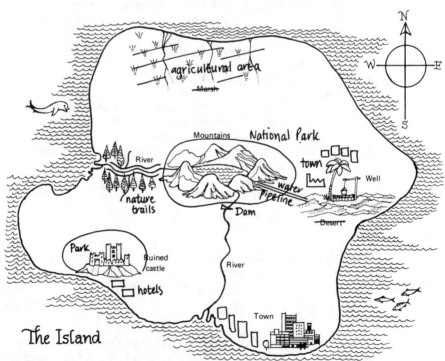

The Island

Such listening exercises based on maps are, again, a feature of many of the books listed under *Task-centred listening* in the *Bibliography*. In this book, examples of maps can be found in Figs. 5, 6 and 24. In preparing names or alterations, the changes can either be marked in on the teacher's copy or, as here, noted down as lists. Suggestions for work on the first two maps have been included in the texts given on pp. 104–6; here are suggestions for the river map shown in Fig. 24:

Names
river – Dab
town – Dabmouth
road – Northway
park – Carlton Park
west farm – Apple Farm
east farm – Downside Farm
bridge – Carlton Bridge
dam – Sherridge Dam
lake – Sherridge Lake
mountain – Mount Hope

Alterations (as result of war/pestilence/emigration)
town – ruined
west farm – gone
park fence – gone
dam – ruined
lake – reverted to river
river – changed course, now flows along road as far as bridge
marshes round estuary

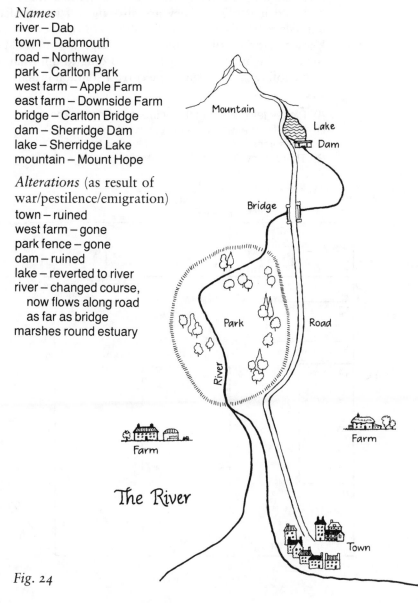

Fig. 24

Ground-plans

Ground-plans are also a kind of map, but a single sketch (Fig. 25a) can be interpreted in many different ways, and correspondingly varied listening tasks can be based on it. Its chief advantage lies in its simplicity: it is very easy to trace and reproduce without necessitating expensive photocopying. Here is a very easy exercise for younger learners. The students are given copies of the plan (with the pools marked in as in Fig. 25b) and told it is a zoo. They are also given a written list of the animals in the zoo – the teacher should of course make sure they know what they all are, and what a 'cage' is – and told to write them in the appropriate spaces according to information given in the following dialogue. The correct solution is marked in Fig. 25c:

A: Please tell me where the animals are in your zoo.
B: Well, tell me what animals you want to see.
A: I love lions.
B: That's easy. The lions are in the biggest cage, the first one you

Fig. 25a

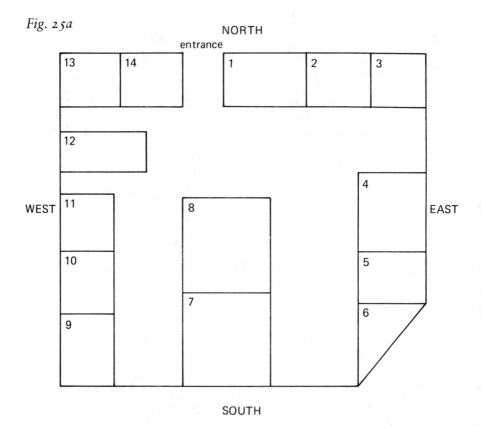

see in front of you as you come in. Behind it is another big cage, the hippos are in that – they have a pool to swim in.

A: What animals are in the smaller cages?

B: Well, near the hippos in the corner is a small cage with a pool in – can you see it?

A: Yes.

B: The dolphins live in that. And next to them is the fox.

A: Only one fox?

B: Yes. Then there are the pelicans; they live between the monkeys and the fox. The monkeys have a bigger cage, they need room to climb.

A: I see. The pelicans have the fox on one side and the monkeys on the other. What about the cages near the entrance?

B: Well, on one side of the entrance are three cages and on the other side – two. Right?

A: Right.

B: Well, in the two cages are giraffes and zebras.

A: Which is which?

B: The giraffes are nearer to the entrance. On the other side of the entrance are the pandas. Then there's an empty cage, then the camels.

Fig. 25b

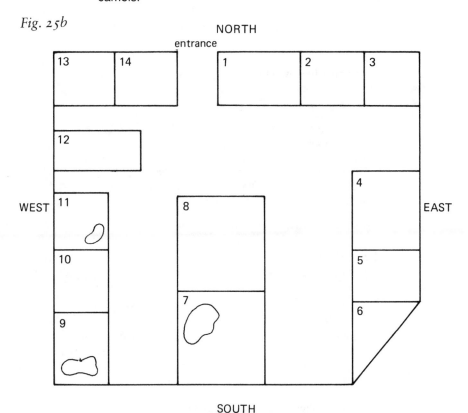

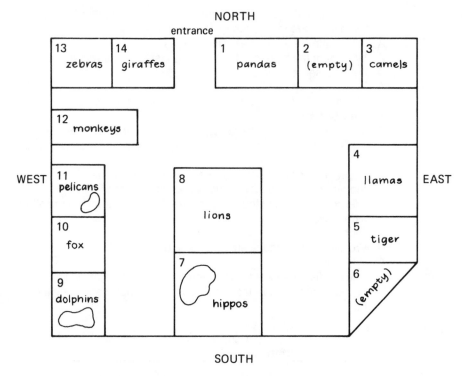

zebras, pelicans, dolphins, hippos, lions, tiger, camels, pandas,
giraffes, monkeys, fox, llamas

Fig. 25c

A: The empty cage is between the pandas and the camels.
B: That's right.
A: There are three more cages you haven't told me about.
B: Oh yes, well, the big cage near the camels has llamas in it. And
behind them is a smaller cage with a tiger. The very smallest cage
in the corner is empty at the moment.

A variation of this zoo exercise, for more advanced learners, is
to give a recorded passage describing changes in the zoo layout.
The students might use the filled-in sketch shown in Fig. 25c as a
basis for corrections; or, if you want to make it really challenging, and if the class has not already done the exercise described
above, they can be given one or two blank sketches like Fig. 25b,
and told to fill in either the final arrangement, or both the final
and the original using only the following information; they may
or may not be given a list of the animals. The passage below is at
intermediate to advanced level, and is based on an idea suggested by Alan Maley:

A: Right, now today we have to decide on some changes in the homes of the animals in our zoo. Mr Jones, please would you explain the details.

B: Yes, well, we'll have to think hard about which animals should go into which enclosures. Firstly, we have bought two new giraffes, and the giraffes' old place next to the entrance isn't big enough any more. I suggest we move them to the other side of the entrance.

C: So what'll happen to the pandas who are there now?

B: They'll move next door to the empty enclosure.

A: And next to them?

B: We'll leave the camels there where they are, they seem to be quite happy.

A: Well, that seems quite reasonable; do you all agree?

C,D: Yes, fine, O.K. . . .

A: Please go on, Mr Jones.

B: There have been some complaints that the lions shouldn't be in the enclosure opposite the entrance – some of the children are frightened as they come in. As we've bought two new elephants, I suggest we put them into there, the children will like them.

D: And move the lions to the enclosure behind?

B: No, lions don't need a pool, and that enclosure's a bit too big for them – as you remember, our third lion died recently, so the two remaining ones can move into a smaller cage. We'll leave the hippos in the big enclosure with the pool, and the lions will go into the cage opposite their old one to the east, next to the tiger.

C: What will we put into the giraffes' old enclosure?

B: The zebras. They're pleasant animals to see near the entrance, and it only means moving them next door. Then we can put the llamas, which are next to the tiger at the moment, by the zebras. They don't really like being next to the tiger, I think they're afraid of him. The triangular cage next to the tiger can stay empty.

A: What about the last four enclosures you haven't mentioned: the dolphins, the pelicans, the fox and the monkeys – leave them as they are?

B: No, well you see there's a problem here too. The pelicans have the fox on one side and the monkeys on the other, and they find both animals very disturbing: the monkeys are noisy and the fox frightens them. They are unhappy, not eating properly – we'll have to do something.

D: Perhaps we could move them to the end, change places with the dolphins; there are pools in both enclosures.

B: Yes, all right. But that still leaves them next to the fox. However, London Zoo want to buy the fox and have offered us a lot of money for him; I suggest we sell him and put our new deer in there instead. Deer don't disturb anyone.

A: Well, thank you Mr Jones. Are we all agreed? Fine. The meeting is closed.

The solution to this is given in Fig. 25d.

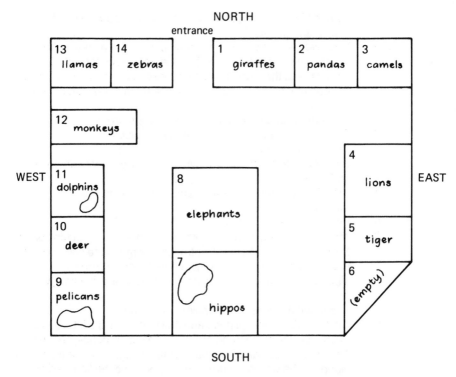

NORTH

entrance

zebras, pelicans, dolphins, hippos, lions, tiger, camels, pandas, giraffes, monkeys, llamas, deer, elephants

Fig. 25d   A further variation is based on the plan as a shopping centre. Students are asked to mark in the kind of shop or the name of the shopkeeper, or both (Fig. 25e). Again there is some writing to be done, so the spoken passage will need to have frequent pauses and reiterations. Names of shops can be shortened or represented by symbols where appropriate; names of people can be jotted in using only the initial letter (intermediate level):

Well, our new shopping centre is finished at last, and I know you are all waiting to hear who's to be where. Get your pencils ready to mark down your locations. Dina, I'm giving you the big site opposite the entrance for your coffee-bar – it's nice and central, so that shoppers will find it convenient to drop in for a cup of coffee or other refreshments. Now the food stores I'm putting in those three sites next to the entrance along the north-eastern wall. Jack, you can sell your fruit and vegetables beside the entrance; and Benny, your bakery is next door. Carole, I'm giving you the corner site for your grocery store. On the other side of the entrance are Tony's gift shop and Ella's toys. Now I know both of you want to be next to the entrance; in the end I decided to give the entrance site to Ella, because her shop will catch the eye of the children as they come in, and with any luck they'll get their parents to spend some money in there. O.K. The big separate site on the western side near Tony goes to Frances for her dress boutique – all right, Frances? Good. South of her there are three smaller sites which will go to Peter for his three businesses: jewellery (better have that near the dress shop, Peter), watches and clocks, and then in the corner the art shop – a nice quiet place for people to look at your pictures and things. Along the eastern wall – we'll give the biggest site to Rosemary, you use that for your book store: I know you'll be selling magazines and stationery as well as books, so you can use the space. Next to Rosemary there's a smaller space – Sheila, you can have that for your kitchen-equipment store. Behind that is a very much smaller triangular room – that'll be the washroom and toilets. Now the big site behind Dina's coffee-bar – we'll give to George for his furniture store – you'll need all that space for your tables and chairs, George.

The same sketch can be used to show the layout of many other kinds of complexes: a school, a museum, a nursing home, offices, an army barracks, stores, botanical gardens. Suggestions for the content of listening passages to go with one or two of these are given below in note form. The teacher can work from these notes as they stand, or insert the information into a copy of

Fig. 25e

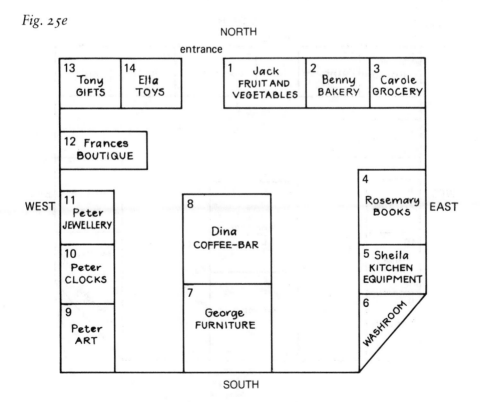

the plan and work from that; she can simply convey the information in her own words, or prepare more elaborate situation-based monologue or dialogue.

The shopping centre
Locations: as in passage above
Changes: Rosemary went bankrupt – left
            Sheila expanded into Rosemary's space
            Tony and Ella quarrelled – so Tony changed places with
                Peter (art)
            Benny and Carole married – merged shops
            Jack died – so Helen took over store
            extra washroom built next to Carole

The nursing home (Fig. 25f)
Locations: 1 caretaker's office   6 Mr Bingly   11 Mrs Ayle
           2 doctor's office   7 kitchen   12 TV room
           3 nurse   8 dining-room   13,
           4 Mr Lee   9 Mrs Dell   14 } bathrooms
           5 Mr Toms   10 Miss Parker
Changes: TV room enlarged – now extends as far as northern wall
            of Mrs Ayle's room

Fig. 25f

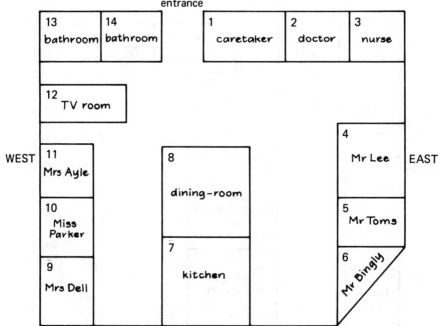

Mr Bingly died
Miss Parker got well – left
wall between Mr Toms and Mr Bingly knocked down
extra room built between 6 and 7 – Mr Hall
extra door opened to outside between 7 and 9
Mrs Dell moved into Miss Parker's room
Miss Ingle arrived – room 11

The school (Fig. 25g)

Locations:
1 art and hand- work room
2 Principal's office
3 secretary
4 Class 3
5 toilets
6 cleaners' room
7 Class 2
8 Class 1
9 Class 4
10 Class 5
11 Class 6
12 staffroom
13 equipment store
14 caretaker

Changes: separate blocks built for classes 1 and 2 so:
art and handwork – to 7
Class 3 – to 8
staffroom – to 1
12 – remedial teaching room
Class 4 – to 4
room 9 – music room
small stage built at east end between 3 and 4

Fig. 25g

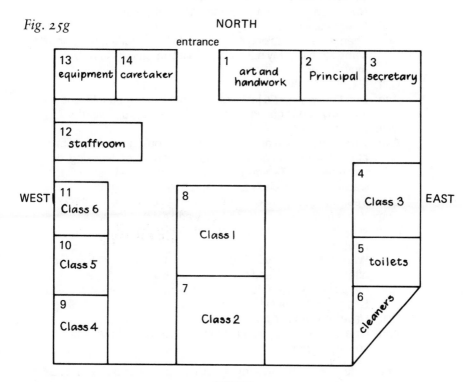

NORTH

Grids

A grid is simply a rectangle marked off into squares and used to display data as illustrated in Fig. 26a–c. The possibilities here are far wider than those of maps or plans, for we are not limited to the proportions of some physical landscape or structure, but can describe many aspects of life, both concrete and abstract.

Here are two people meeting after not having seen each other for some time, exchanging news about each other and about a mutual acquaintance (intermediate level):

Ann: Cliff! I haven't seen you since we finished college. How's things? Where are you living? What are you doing?

Cliff: Ann! I hardly recognized you! You've let your hair grow. It makes you look older.

Ann: Come on ! I'm not that much older!

Cliff: You must be twenty-seven.

Ann: And you're two years younger, and you look exactly the same as ever. What are you doing?

Cliff: Teaching, what else?

Ann: How's it going – where?

Cliff: I still live in London, teach in a comprehensive school there. Are you teaching too?

Ann: No, I got married last year and had a baby recently –

Cliff: Congratulations!

Ann: Thanks – so I'm taking the year off to look after the baby and do some studying. My husband got a job in Cardiff, so we've moved there.

Cliff: Like it?

Ann: Don't know yet, I've just started to get to know people, and with the baby I don't get about much. How about you? Married?

Cliff: Not yet.

Ann: I'm surprised. We always used to say you'd get married first of all of us, you're so good-looking. Talking of good-looking, do you remember Tammy? The beautiful girl from Bristol? She was in the same class as me at school.

Cliff: Yes. She got married at the end of the course, didn't she?

Ann: Yes, and had two children, a boy and a girl.

Cliff: What's she doing, looking after the children, being a housewife?

Ann: Who, Tammy? Never. That's a super-feminist family. He looks after the children, and she works full-time; she edits a magazine, writes articles for the newspapers, very successful. She's been on television once or twice.

Cliff: Have you seen any of the others?

Ann: One or two – let's go for a cup of coffee somewhere, and I'll tell you about them.

The students may be presented with an empty grid as in Fig. 26a, or with an inaccurately filled-in one, as in Fig. 26b, which they

Name	Age	Occupation	Appearance	Town	Family

Fig. 26a

Name	Age	Occupation	Appearance	Town	Family
Cliff	27	teacher	tall, dark, handsome	Cardiff	married
Ann	29	teacher	long hair	London	married, one child
Tammy	27	writer	beautiful	Bristol	married, three children

Fig. 26b

have to correct. In either case the correct solution should come out something like Fig. 26c.

Admittedly this is not a very exciting subject, though classes I have tried it out on seem to find it absorbing enough. The grid technique can be extended to more dramatic and entertaining situations – a murder story, for example. In the following exercise the students are detectives listening to a recorded report of the evidence and taking notes in grid form on the alibis of the various suspects. Each of the members of the household of the dead man has a story to cover his or her activities on the night of

Name	Age	Occupation	Appearance	Town	Family
Ann	27	looking afer baby, studying	long hair (looks older)	Cardiff	married, one child
Cliff	25	teacher	good-looking	London	unmarried
Tammy	27	edits, writes, appears on TV	beautiful	Bristol?	married, two children

Fig. 26c

the murder. The 'detectives' have to mark in the various stories in the appropriate places on their grids. The names of the people may or may not be written in previously. Again, this is at intermediate level:

Report of evidence given by members of the Jones household in the Jones murder case. Lord Percy Jones was murdered in the garden of his house some time between 7.0 p.m. and midnight of 15 June. The suspects described their activities on that night as follows: Lady Jones was having her dinner until eight, she then sat playing the piano to her daughter Mary until nine, watched television and went to bed a little before midnight. Tom Jones had dinner with his mother and sister, but afterwards went out for a drive and didn't get back until late. Mary had a headache and went to bed after listening to her mother playing the piano, but she couldn't sleep. She heard her brother come in at eleven; at twelve she decided that a walk in the fresh air would help her, and it was then she discovered her father's body. Her screams awakened Sir Harry, the dead man's brother, and he came down to her and telephoned the police. Sir Harry himself had quarrelled with his brother just before dinner – so neither of them came down to the meal. Sir Harry says he was in his room all evening, but Jeff, the servant, claims he met him in the garden at about supper-time. Jane, the maid, served dinner and then Jeff helped her to clear the table and wash up, and they went to the cinema at nine, getting back at eleven-thirty. They had a cup of tea in the kitchen before going to bed just before midnight.

The completed grid is given in Fig. 27.

A follow-up could be a discussion to invent further necessary details (How did the victim die? What were his relations with

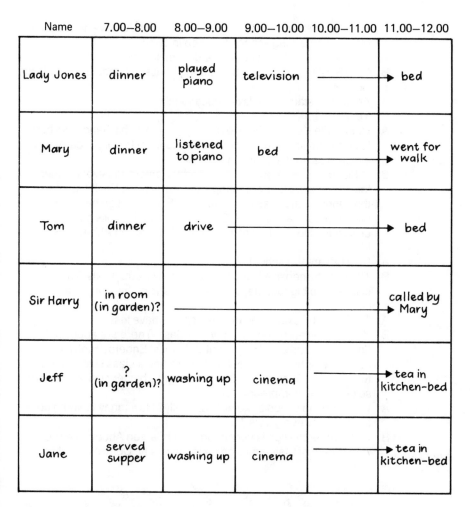

Name	7.00–8.00	8.00–9.00	9.00–10.00	10.00–11.00	11.00–12.00
Lady Jones	dinner	played piano	television	———————▶	bed
Mary	dinner	listened to piano	bed	——————▶	went for walk
Tom	dinner	drive	——————————————▶		bed
Sir Harry	in room (in garden)?	————————————————————————▶			called by Mary
Jeff	? (in garden)?	washing up	cinema	——————▶	tea in kitchen-bed
Jane	served supper	washing up	cinema	——————▶	tea in kitchen-bed

Fig. 27

members of the family? What motive could anyone have had?) and to suggest a solution.

The subjects of a grid do not of course have to be people. Here is a passage comparing different schools in an English town (intermediate to advanced level):

A: Well, before we decide we're going to live in Enderby, we really ought to have a look at the schools; we want the children to have a good secondary education, so we'd better see what's available.

B: They gave me some information at the office, and I took notes. It appears there are five secondary schools in Enderby: three state schools and two private.

A: I don't know if we want private schools, do we?

B: I don't think so, but we'll look at them anyway. There's St Mary's, that's a Catholic school for girls, and Carlton Abbey – that's a very old boys' boarding school, founded in 1672.

A: Do any other schools have boarding facilities?

B: Yes, St Mary's has a small boarding house, as does Enderby High School.

A: Are all the state schools coeducational?

B: Yes, it seems so.

A: I think little Keith is going to be very good with his hands, we ought to send him to a school with good vocational training – carpentry, electronics, that sort of thing.

B: In that case we're best off at Enderby Comprehensive, I gather they have excellent workshops and instructors. But it says here that Donwell also has good facilities. Enderby High has a little, but they're mostly academic – 50 per cent of their pupils go on to university. No vocational training at all at Carlton Abbey or St Mary's.

A: How big are the schools?

B: The comprehensive is the biggest, about 1,000 pupils. Their classes are big too, they have an average of thirty pupils to a class.

A: That's a lot. I expect the private schools have less.

B: Yes, they average only twenty to a class. There are about 200 boys at Carlton and 150 girls at St Mary's. Enderby High looks about the right size – about 500 pupils and a class size of about twenty-four. Donwell has 600, and slightly bigger classes, but not so big as the comprehensive's.

A: What are the schools like academically? How many children go on to university every year?

B: Well, Enderby High is very good – and Carlton Abbey even better, 70 per cent of their pupils go on to university. Donwell is not so

Fig. 28

	Private/ State	Girls/Boys/ Coed	Religious	No. of pupils	Boarders	% going to university	Vocational training	Class size
Enderby High School	S	coed	✓	500	✓	50%	a little	24
Carlton Abbey	P	boys	✓	200	✓	70%	X	20
Donwell School	S	coed	✓	600	X	8%	✓	25–29
Enderby Comprehensive	S	coed	✓	1,000	X	10%	✓	30
St. Mary's	P	girls	Catholic	150	✓	10%	X·	20

good, only 8 per cent, and the comprehensive and St Mary's not
much more – about 10 per cent.

A: Well, they certainly seem like quite good schools. But we'll have to
find out more than statistics before we can decide.

The students are given a grid with column headings and the
names of the schools (optionally) inserted. The finished exercise
should look something like Fig. 28. Again, the teacher can
prepare the grid either blank or already filled in with faulty
information to be corrected.

The basic content of most informative listening passages (the
news, weather forecasts, financial or sports reports, transport
schedules, plans and programmes) can be expressed in the form
of a grid, though some of the spaces may often be left blank. It is
simpler on the whole to take such a passage as a basis and work
out a grid from it than to make up a grid and then compose a
passage (though of course both are possible). The flight schedules shown on p. 92 for example might be expressed as
follows:

Flight No.	From	To	Landing	Taking Off
SK 143	Oslo		X	
BA 501	Geneva, Paris		X	
TW 304		New York		X
BA 692		Madrid		X

As regards published material: occasional such exercises appear
in most task-based listening comprehension books, but probably
the best source is *Listening links* by Marion Geddes and Gill
Sturtridge, most of whose exercises can be presented as 'straight'
grid-based listening as well as in the more complex way
suggested. Further examples in this book can be found on pp.
154, 155, 157 together with the corresponding grids in Figs.
32b, 33, 34.

Family trees

This has become a favourite type of diagram in communicative
English teaching, for both listening and speaking exercises.
Family relationships and histories are interesting subjects, or can
easily be made so. However, the family-tree diagram is rather
more difficult to assimilate at a glance than maps or grids:
relationships such as uncle or cousin take longer to work out
than one might expect, so that stories or descriptions of families

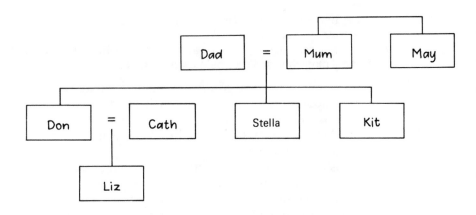

Dad, Kit, Mum, May, Don, Cath, Liz

Fig. 29

have to be taken slowly with frequent pauses and repetitions. Here is a very simple example for elementary classes. Notice that the names are kept short to facilitate quick writing, and are printed as a list under the blank diagram so that all the pupil has to do is recognize and insert them correctly. Also, the name of the central character is inserted in advance (Fig. 29):

A: Hi, you're new here, aren't you? What's your name?
B: Stella.
A: Want to come and play?
B: I'd like to, but I can't. My Mum says I've got to stay and help her. It's my brother's birthday and we're having a party.
A: Oh, you've got a brother, have you?
B: I've got two brothers. Kit, the one with the birthday, he's only little, he's four. I've got a big brother who's married, his name's Don.
A: Does your brother Don live near here?
B: Yes, not very far away. Cath – that's his wife – she works in the sweetshop over there. They've got a new baby called Liz, I mean Elizabeth really, but we call her Liz.
A: Is that your Mum over there calling you?
B: No, that's my Aunt May, my Mum's sister. I'd better go. Bye.
A: Bye.

A more intricate family tree is shown in Fig. 30. The story that goes with it, for a more advanced class, follows:

Let me tell you about the royal family of Trembia. As you know, John made himself king in 1910; no one knows who his father was, but anyway he married Fay from his home village . . . I don't think she was ever really happy as queen, but she had three children. One of them died young, poor thing, Jack his name was . . . yes, Jack . . . a good-looking little boy, judging by portraits. His older sister, Mary,

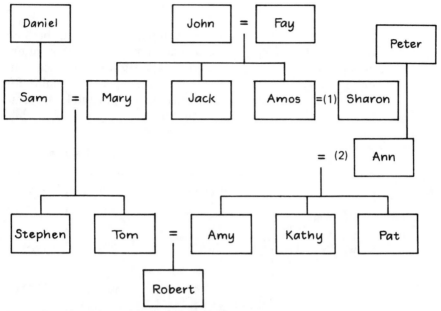

Daniel, Sam, Stephen, Tom, Mary, John, Jack, Amy, Robert,
Kathy, Amos, Fay, Peter, Ann, Pat, Sharon

Fig. 30   married Sam, the son of King Daniel of Shambia, so that was a very
useful marriage, politically. The third child of John and Fay was called
Amos – he was made king after his father died. He married twice. His
first wife, Sharon, was a lovely girl, but she had no children, so he had
her killed. She had been so popular with the people that there was
minor rebellion when it happened . . . there were riots, and in the end
a mob attacked the royal palace and set it on fire. Amos managed to
escape to a friend of his, Lord Peter, whose daughter he later
married. He wasn't a very pleasant person, but I believe Ann was quite
happy with him. They had children, but never the son that Amos had
wanted. Meanwhile Amos's nephew Stephen became king and ruled
for many years, but he never married, or, as far as I know, had
children. His younger brother Tom did marry, his cousin Amy, whose
sisters Kathy and Pat remained with their grandfather Peter, and
never married. The present king of Trembia and Shambia is Sam's
grandson, Robert.

This exercise can be made much easier by inserting four or five
of the names correctly beforehand; it can be made more difficult
by omitting the ready-made list of names below, and even more
so by omitting the entire diagram and making the students draw
it themselves from scratch, with only the listening passage to
guide them. In this case, of course, the description will need to
be expanded, taken very slowly, and repeated two or three
times.

Graphs

Very similar exercises to those exemplified above can be built round graphs, which provide an excellent base for information-giving, especially for more academic classes or those concentrating on English for science and technology. We could, for instance, take the two graphs shown in Fig. 31a and let students fill in the details missing from their copy (Fig. 31b), while

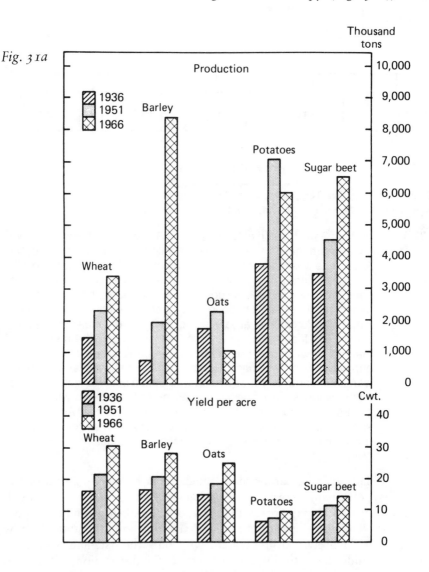

Chart 13: Production and yields of certain crops in Great Britain

listening to the information given below (intermediate/advanced level):

Well, these two graphs show how certain branches of English agriculture were doing over a thirty-year period, from 1936 to 1966. Let's look at the top graph first. You can see that it shows the total production of various crops in the years 1936, 1951 and 1966. The crops shown here are, reading from left to right: wheat, barley, oats, potatoes and sugar beet. Along the vertical axis at the right you can

Fig. 3 1b

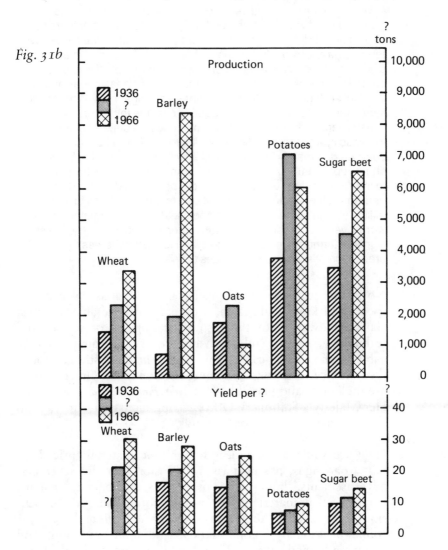

Chart 13: Production and yields of certain crops in Great Britain

see numbers – 1,000, 2,000 and so on: these represent thousands of tons of crops, so that the number 1,000 in fact represents a thousand thousand, that is a million, tons.

The bottom graph deals with the same crops for the same years, but relates to the productivity of the agriculture, that is, how much the farmers are managing to produce per acre. The yield per acre is measured in hundredweight – that's the abbreviation cwt you can see at the top of the right-hand vertical axis (in England a hundredweight is one twentieth of a ton).

Well, in general as you can see, things have been improving on both counts. If you look at the bottom graph you'll see that there has been a steady increase in yield per acre for all these crops. However, farmers have obviously increased their know-how and efficiency in grain-crop production rather more than in root-crops: if you look carefully you'll see that the increase in yield of wheat, barley and oats is relatively higher than that of potatoes and sugar beet. Wheat yield increased particularly, almost doubling over the thirty-year period.

As regards total production, the increase isn't quite so uniform. The increase in wheat production is similar to that in yield per acre, and so could be due mainly to higher productivity – but look at the barley: that shoots up in 1966 to something like $8\frac{1}{2}$ million tons, which would seem to indicate that farmers are using more of their land to grow barley, perhaps at the expense of oats, whose production drops to about a million tons in 1966, in spite of higher yield per acre. Potatoes, which were a very successful crop in 1951, drop perceptibly in 1966, also a sign that farmers are devoting less land to them, whereas the production of sugar beet continues to rise.

No further examples of graphs are given here, as this is a very specialized kind of diagram, not necessarily suitable for most classes. However, for those studying English for science and technology, or for children who are also learning scientific subjects, the teacher can lift this kind of material straight out of their science textbooks and improvise comment. Other sources are the books and pamphlets (such as *Facts in focus*) issued by Her Majesty's Stationery Office, giving factual information on various social and economic trends.

Here are some further ideas for graphic material: price-lists, bills, road-signs, passport visas, television or radio schedules, advertisements, book-lists, flow charts, sociograms, menus. Some excellent material to use as bases for listening comprehension tasks can be found in *Cue for a drill* and *Cue for communication* by Shiona Harkess and John Eastwood. And many ready-made exercises can be taken from the books listed in the *Bibliography* under *Task-centred listening*.

5.3   Listening and making longer responses

The exercises suggested in the previous section demanded from the learner brief and simple verbal or non-verbal responses to each bit of information as it was received, and the function of these responses was primarily to indicate comprehension. For the following exercises, in contrast, the learner uses relatively long units of language (written, read or spoken) in his responses; and he has to be able not only to understand what he hears, but also to reproduce, answer, expand or summarize it as required. Thus, whereas the brief responses in previous exercises were more or less convergent (there was only one 'right' response in each case), those in this section are typically open-ended (excepting those based on repetition or multiple-choice techniques), and the student can exercise his ability to produce spoken or written language.

The first few suggestions are based on the reproduction of short units of heard speech; but as we go on, detailed grasp of such units becomes less important, and a 'holistic' approach is adopted: that is, learners are asked to relate to the general sense of a whole sequence of utterances.

One of the most obvious ways to find out if you have been understood is to ask your hearer: 'Well, what did I say?' If he has understood, and has a fair active command of the language, he should be able to give you an accurate reconstruction of what you said. In the classroom we use three main kinds of reproduction exercises: repetition, paraphrase and translation, each of which may consist of either oral or written language (the first three sections of 5.3).

Another technique which is used a great deal to check comprehension is the question-and-answer. Here we differentiate between the spoken question used *as text* in itself (*Answering questions*), and the spoken or written question used simply as a check on the understanding of a previously administered listening text (*Answering comprehension questions on texts*).

The last three sections of 5.3 are taken up with exercises that tackle the problem of coping with redundancy and 'noise'. The learner is given practice in extracting the essential information from listening passages some parts of which he may not understand and others he can safely ignore or 'skim'. In exercises in the last three sections of 5.3 the learner is asked to predict what is to come, to reconstruct missing information, and to summarize the main points of fairly discursive passages.

Repetition and dictation

If we ask students to repeat what they have heard, we may not be testing comprehension at all, but merely accurate perception, retention and mimicry. Most people can imitate what they hear fairly well without understanding, provided the items are short and not too much time elapses between hearing and repeating (see p. 37). However, it is certainly untrue to say that repetition has no value at all as a comprehension exercise. Once the material heard consists of a series of complete utterances which the student has to memorize and then repeat after a short but appreciable interval, comprehension must come into play. Try listening to five seconds of coherent discourse in a language you know nothing of. You will be unable to repeat it, even though many of the individual sounds may be familiar. Now listen to five seconds of speech in a language you speak fluently, and you will find you can repeat it with appropriate stress and intonation with little or no difficulty. In other words, longer coherent passages of discourse can be accurately repeated only if there is a high level of comprehension on the part of the repeater. Thus, in order to reproduce a sentence, learners will listen carefully not only for the sounds but also for the meaning; and this, I think, justifies our using repetition as an occasional listening comprehension exercise. At the elementary level, students can be asked to repeat simple exchanges like:

'Where are you going?'
'Outside – are you coming?'

or:

'Give me that book please.'
'Which, this one? Here you are.'

More advanced students can cope with things like:

'I don't think you can have noticed that Bob has been trying to attract your attention for the last ten minutes.'

Students can be asked to reproduce the material immediately or after an interval. The time-lapse allows the factor of comprehension to play an even greater part, since we remember, as we perceive, what we understand far better than what we do not. If we give seven or eight sentences to be memorized and then recalled, we shall find that the sentences that students do not understand so well are the ones to be forgotten, and the most easily comprehensible are the first to be remembered.

One disadvantage of repetition exercises that has already been mentioned is that they are very time-consuming if the teacher wants to check each student's performance. A way of getting over this is to ask students to write down what they have heard instead of saying it aloud; the written versions can be checked later either by the teacher or, perhaps more productively, by the students themselves using a correct version. This is, of course, the dictation, which can be used to check accurate perception and comprehension as well as spelling. If a student has perceived correctly, he will represent the sounds by appropriate letters, but may not get the word-division or spelling right. If he has both perceived and understood, he will get the sound–letter correspondence and the word-divisions, and is likely to make fewer spelling mistakes.

The relationship between repetition and comprehension is of course two-way: not only do we repeat things better if we understand them, but also understand and learn things better if we repeat them. The audio-lingual methods of foreign-language teaching (that is, methods in which a large proportion of student work consists of mimicry, memorization and stimulus–response drills) rely heavily upon this principle; and although such methods have become less popular in recent years, the principle remains true, at least in my experience. A minute or two of brisk repetition exercises based on newly taught lexis or grammatical structures can improve absorption of this material as well as giving listening comprehension and pronunciation practice.

Paraphrase

Repetition is the reproduction of spoken material in its original form. Paraphrase is reproduction of such material in a different form – that is, using different words of the same language to express the same ideas. Obviously, there is no possibility here of mindless mimicry: on the contrary, the teacher should be aware that paraphrase is a relatively difficult exercise even for native speakers, and only intelligent and fairly proficient students may be expected to do it successfully and get useful practice thereby.

Long passages can be broken down into short 'bits' and each 'bit' paraphrased as it is heard; consider the following:

Original: After we'd seen the film, we felt so disturbed we just couldn't go to bed.
Paraphrase: That film was so exciting we couldn't sleep after it.
Original: So we sat up talking about it until 3.0 a.m.
Paraphrase: We went on discussing it until three in the morning.
Original: I mean, makes you wonder, a film like that.
Paraphrase: Films like that make you think about things.
or:

Original: Jackie, what's the time?
Paraphrase: He asked Jackie what the time was.

Original: Five, I think.
Paraphrase: She said she thought it was five o'clock.
Original: Well, come on then, let's go.
Paraphrase: He said they had to go.
Original: Where to?
Paraphrase: She asked where they had to go to.

One criticism of these exercises that springs to mind immediately is that the paraphrase appears to be very faulty. In several cases the original phrases or parts of them are repeated, not paraphrased; and sometimes the paraphrase seems to be a rather inaccurate reproduction of the sense of the original. But the point is that we are not aiming here for an accurate or elegant rewording; all we want is a clear signal that the student has grasped the sense of what was said and can express it roughly in his own words. From that point of view these renderings, inexact as they are, are perfectly adequate. There is also the aspect of efficient use of time. If we spend long correcting and polishing a good paraphrase, we may contribute something to a student's academic knowledge of the language, but little or nothing to the improvement of his comprehension skills. In other words, we must have clear in our minds the distinction between literary paraphrase – done for the purpose of intensive academic language study and best based on a written text – and communicative paraphrase, done to check general comprehension and language-use, and best based on spoken discourse.

Another criticism, which applies to the second exercise shown above, is its heavy reliance on indirect speech, a structure which is often very difficult for learners. But when we paraphrase in real life, we are very often describing what someone else has said, and therefore do often use indirect speech; and exercises like this give good practice in it.

There is a third problem about basing paraphrase exercises on such short utterances, and that is that the temptation to repeat is overwhelming. If you have just heard and understood a sentence and are asked what was said, it takes a conscious effort to reproduce it in different words; the natural tendency is to repeat more or less word for word. Obviously the paraphrasing *can* be done, and can give useful practice; but perhaps we can help students to do it by giving them some acceptable justification for using other words. For example, if we present them with a formal version of a text in fairly advanced language, we can ask them to paraphrase it in simple informal terms as they would if explaining the content to a less advanced learner. This accords also with the general truth that most learners can understand much more difficult language than they can produce. An example:

Original: The performance was attended by a large audience.
Paraphrase: Lots of people came to see the show.
Original: And there was loud applause at its conclusion.
Paraphrase: And clapped loudly at the end.
Original: However, the opinion of the critics did not accord with that of the public.
Paraphrase: But the critics didn't think it was as good as the public did.

But the most obvious way to get over the temptation to repeat word for word is to abandon, at least in part, our preference for having students respond at frequent intervals while they are listening and let them hear a longer stretch of discourse, responding only at the end. For this we need to have a listening passage that is readily grasped as a whole; that is, it should be coherent, not too long, and with clear overall development: a story, for example, a news item, an argument or a description. The students' grasp of such passages can be helped by visuals. They can, for instance, listen to the story about the dog on the television aerial (pp. 56–7) while following it according to the pictures in Fig. 4, and then reconstruct what they have heard in their own words, using the pictures as a guide. The paraphrase will naturally be a much rougher rendering than in the exercises described previously, and the students' statements may also not be in the same order as those of the original.

Without visual aids it is a little more difficult to reproduce a heard passage. Suppose they hear a short talk like this (advanced level):

The common marmoset and many of the others have a system whereby they travel and live in large groups, and in any one of these groups only one female breeds. So that she will keep on breeding – she can produce twins twice a year (they have a gestation period – pregnancy – that lasts four and a half months); and then all the members of that group will help to carry those babies, to take them around, but no other female will breed. And it's unique among mammals, with the exception perhaps of wolves, and some very small animals called naked mole rats, that one dominant female will 'turn off' all the other females. And it's just as well, perhaps, because if these animals kept to their reproductive potential, and all of them would produce two sets of twins a year, the Amazon would just be weighed down with marmosets. It's very interesting that many animals have a natural control system which keeps their population in balance with the environment.

(Transcript from 'Nature notebook', BBC World Service, 11 August 1982)

Students can then be asked to tell the teacher what they have
found out about marmosets, at random, until they have recon-
structed most of the information (they may need to have been
told beforehand that the marmoset is a small South American
monkey!). Their memory can be aided by cues from the teacher:
not questions, but one-word reminders, round which they can
build their paraphrases of the original relevant part of the
passage. For example:

Teacher cue: female
Student response: The female can have twins twice a year.
           or: Only one female in a group has babies.
           or: The female has a pregnancy of four and
                a half months.
Teacher cue: group
Student response: Marmosets go around in large groups.
           or: In each group only one female reproduces.
           or: All the marmosets in a group help to look
                after the young.

Oral paraphrase exercises are best done as a free exchange full
class activity; that is to say, the teacher gives the cue, either
general ('What was all that about?') or specific (like the one-
word reminders above), then lets students put up their hands to
volunteer responses, additions and corrections. She may then
give her own summary of the students' suggestions in order to
finish up. The entire exercise will probably not take longer than
five minutes.

If we ask students to write down their paraphrases instead of
saying them out loud, we may get more exact and careful results,
and be able to check them later. On the other hand, the exercise
becomes much more long-drawn-out and tedious, and students
cannot benefit from each other's suggestions. More important,
the kind of language students are normally able to comprehend
aurally is of a far higher level than that which they can write
themselves, so that a writing exercise of this kind may be
disproportionately difficult.

Translation

Translation is a kind of paraphrase – that is, it is a rewording of
the sense of an original text; and as we shall see, many of the
comments made about paraphrase as a listening comprehension
activity are relevant also to translation. The big difference is, of
course, that the new words are in another language: there is little
or no possibility of repetition, and in many ways the whole
process is much easier.

Translation is a rather unpopular technique in the foreign-language classroom these days. Over-use of it tends to induce learners to see the foreign language primarily in terms of their own, and delays their grasp of it as a new means of communication in its own right. Translation gives little practice in communication skills, and can waste lesson time letting students use their own, known, language when they need the time to practise the new one. And 'real' translation is of course a highly skilled technique in itself, largely irrelevant to a foreign-language course.

Nevertheless the proper, controlled use of certain types of translation techniques can be of great value in foreign-language teaching. We should not aim for elegant, accurate renderings of long passages into another language – this is indeed very difficult and time-consuming and contributes relatively little to the learning of the foreign language as such. But translation can and should be used simply as a comprehension aid and check; done by teacher or students, a quick, rough translation into the native language can save minutes of fumbling search for a comprehensible explanation in English – and ensure understanding as well. In any case, students often look for, and find, translations on their own; adults particularly seem to need the security of knowing their native-language equivalent, however imprecise, of what they learn.

Many of the exercises used for paraphrasing are suitable also for translation. The exercises given on pp. 129–30, for example, may be translated instead of paraphrased. In the longer passage, about marmosets (p. 131), we would not expect students to translate sentence by sentence, but would simply ask something like: 'Well, what was all that about?', or 'Now, what can you tell me about marmosets?', allowing them to volunteer all the information they could remember, in their own language.

Students also, obviously, write their own language more quickly and easily than they write the foreign one. Thus 'Jot down everything you have found out about the marmosets from what you've heard', though a rather laborious task to do in English, may be a perfectly feasible one if done in the native language.

The same kinds of listening materials that have been recommended for paraphrasing can be used for translation.

Answering questions

Receiving an appropriate reply to a question is another very obvious signal that the question has been understood; and the question–answer sequence occurs commonly in real-life situations. Question–answer is also one of the most popular teaching procedures used in the classroom – and not just in foreign-language lessons. Questions are commonly used in the teaching of any subject to get students' minds working along the right lines, to stimulate curiosity, to elicit information, to test knowledge and so on.

It is sometimes argued that most classroom questions are not 'genuine' questions in that the asker (the teacher) is not asking about something she really does not know and wants to find out; she usually knows the answer perfectly well. And 'non-genuine' questions, it is claimed, should not form part of fluency practice (whether of listening or of speaking) in communicative language teaching. (There are even those who go so far as to say that such questions should not be used in language teaching at all, though I have no idea how they think this is to be achieved!) I am rather dubious about this theory. First, it seems to me that there are plenty of perfectly genuine real-life situations where the asker knows the answer to the question, or does not care what it is, and is asking it for other reasons, no less valid. Examples of these are the questions asked by a radio or television interviewer, questions asked of a witnesss in a trial, rhetorical questions ('Don't you agree?'), 'phatic' questions ('Isn't it a lovely day?'), requests ('Can you pass the sugar?'), testing questions inside and outside the classroom (like the optician's 'What is this row of letters?'), and many others. In fact, I am not at all sure that the majority of real-life questions are in fact 'genuine' in the sense defined above. Second, even if questions that really request new information are seen as in some way of a higher calibre of 'communicativity', this does not mean that other kinds of questions are not communicative or that the asker does not want or deserve an appropriate response from the person addressed. The only type of question–answer series that does not give communication practice is mechanical pattern-drill, where learners can give the right answer without understanding ('Is he going?' 'Yes, he is going.' 'Is he singing?' 'Yes, he is singing.').

I would say that any series of teacher-questions followed by student-answers will give good communication practice provided that the questions are such as to require an explicit response (not necessarily verbal, but at least observable, like a nod), and that they are likely to be answered correctly only if they have been understood. A further condition, if there is to be effective listening practice, is that the questions should not be displayed to the students in written form; too often all the teacher does is to read them aloud while the students follow, so that the listening practice they get is not very useful – they hardly need to use their ears at all.

Most question–answer procedures have other objectives besides listening practice: comprehension of a text (as described in *Answering comprehension questions on texts*), revision of language material, testing. However, there are some in which listening practice is the primary aim. (The ones described here are based on 'Wh' questions: 'Yes/no' questions are merely another variation of true/false statements whose use has been described on pp. 77–80.)

There is, for example, the general knowledge quiz, whose answers are usually fairly short and can be volunteered orally or jotted down ('Who is the President of the United States?' 'What is the biggest animal on earth?'). Other sets of questions can be based on what students are currently studying in other subjects. Or the teacher can interview students about themselves ('Where are you from?' 'What do you like doing?').

Visuals, again, can be used as a basis for questioning. It is easy to imagine the simple questions that could be based on the pictures given in this book. More difficult questions can be formulated round the diagrammatic material. Exercises like this can be made more challenging and game-like by letting students look at the material and then either concealing it or asking them to close their eyes. They then have to answer the questions from memory.

Finally there is the topic-centred question–answer process, where the answers are liable to be longer and the connection between one answer and the next question closer. The teacher takes a topic, either factual (for example 'our town' or 'professions') or a matter of opinion (such as a topical social issue), and asks the students questions about it: 'When was this town established?' 'What are its major industries?' 'What is a "skilled" profession?' 'What professions are best paid?' 'Do you think comprehensive schooling is a good idea?' 'Why (not)?' This activity is, of course, only one step away from the full debate, the main difference being that here the conversation is still in the form of a structured 'ping-pong' exchange between teacher and students, rather than an open discussion with free participation.

Since question–answer procedures are so widely used in the classroom, most teachers find it relatively easy to improvise questions even without notes to help them. Only in exercises based on general knowledge or on other school subjects will the teacher find that a brief written cue for each question will help her to administer the exercise smoothly.

Answering comprehension questions on texts

The activity discussed here has been perhaps the most widely used listening comprehension technique for intermediate and advanced classes. Students listen to a passage of about 300 to 500 words, which is nearly always spoken prose: an excerpt from a book or article read aloud. They then answer questions on it which may be 'straight' questions, but are nowadays more usually multiple-choice. A typical procedure is for the students to listen to the passage once without looking at the questions, then to look over the questions, then to hear the passage again with the questions before them, and finally fill in the answers.

This type of exercise is rather more academic and demands considerably more effort and concentration than most of those described hitherto. For one thing, the passages are very long and there is a large amount of information to be stored in the students' memory. For another, the questions are written and there is the extra load of reading (in multiple-choice questions) and writing (in other types). Lastly, there is the aspect of inference and deduction. Questions in this type of exercise are rarely formulated using the words of the original text, and they often require students to have understood the implications of what they have heard as well as its surface meaning. Here is an extract from one such exercise:

On the evening of December 23rd we were waiting in the front room, which looked very nice and warm. We only use it when people come, or perhaps in summer, for it's too cold, but now we had the fire going in the open fireplace. We were waiting for a farmer and his wife who lived in Cornwall. My wife had been evacuated there during the war, and since our marriage they've sent a chicken each Christmas and I've given them a bottle of sherry.

1 The story takes place
   a) on a summer evening.
   b) on a cold day.
   c) on a warm night.
   d) just before Christmas.

2 The family use the front room
   a) as their living room.
   b) when they have visitors.
   c) only in summer.
   d) only in winter.

3 They were waiting for
 a) some friends.
 b) some relations.
 c) some business acquaintances.
 d) their children.

(From *First Certificate English 4: listening comprehension* by W. S. Fowler)

This is not a difficult passage; but notice the kind of deduction – albeit simple – that the students are required to make. They are asked to identify the date not as 'December 23rd' as in the text, but as it relates to the coming festival. They are given the history of the relationship between the family and their visitors and then asked to define under which category the latter fall. The front room is used, according to the passage 'when people come or perhaps in summer', and the students then have to choose between the two likely-looking answers 'when they have visitors' and 'only in summer'; it requires an accurate memory and careful deduction from the original information to opt for 'when they have visitors'.

In short, such exercises are a test of memory, intelligence and careful reading as much as of listening comprehension, and may not therefore be appropriate for younger pupils or for those whose reading is much behind their oral skills.

Their usefulness as a component of classroom listening practice is doubtful. They are nearly always based on spoken prose, which, as we have seen, accounts for only a small proportion of the kind of language occurring in listening situations; the actual listening, as shown above, tends to take second place to memory, logical deduction and reading; and the whole activity is very far removed from any real-life situation I can think of.

However, such activities should not be written off as useless. If properly administered they can be made more effective as classroom exercises, and even as conventionally presented they can be useful as advanced tests. They are, for one thing, very convenient to administer and mark. If a set, recorded or read text is used there is no problem of variety or mistakes in delivery, and the multiple-choice questionnaire, if carefully worded, ensures objectivity of marking.* Further, it may be argued that a student taking an examination in general English

---

* But most multiple-choice questionnaires do have one interesting flaw: about two-thirds of the right options are usually also the longest ones. So a student who knows this fact can pass most multiple-choice tests without knowing the answers. Test-composers – take note!

proficiency may perfectly reasonably be required to use his reading and writing skills in demonstrating he has heard rightly; and at this level it is also fair, I think, to test his memory and intelligent analysis of what he has heard; after all, just understanding something is useless unless we can remember and use it to draw relevant conclusions. It is also reasonable to deny the student the physical presence of the speaker in a test situation. This may be relatively unusual in real life, but it does test the student's aural perception and comprehension; if he can listen and understand 'blind', he will certainly be able to do so when aided by visual clues.

Similar reasoning does not however apply to the use of written prose as the text of the listening passages. It is by no means certain that a student who can understand such passages can also understand most spontaneous speech. There is of course a correlation between the two, but, as many foreign students have found to their cost, it is much lower than might be expected. The reasons for using such texts nevertheless are mainly practical. It is comparatively simple to prepare them and control their quality and level, far more difficult to plan and prepare a series of informal spontaneous passages of discourse in such a way that they conform consistently to a certain standard; so that most teachers and testers prefer to use the conventional prose text. However, some sort of compromise should be attainable. The passages used, if not improvised, could at least be taken from discourse meant to be spoken (drama, rhetoric, monologue) and delivered in an approximation to colloquial style.

If we wish to use the same activities as a basis for classroom practice then we should try to make them more relevant, nearer to real-life listening, less academic. Obviously, examples of spoken discourse should be used as text rather than read-aloud prose; and if listening is the main objective, then it seems reasonable to suggest that questions should be spoken rather than written. They should also be delivered as ordinary questions rather than multiple-choice ones; the latter, after all, are very artificial, very awkward to deliver orally and listen to, and have no particular advantage other than objectivity of assessment in testing – which is a minor consideration in the context of classroom practice. The comprehension questions should, if specific, be asked at intervals *during* the text, immediately before or after the particular passages they refer to. If asked before, then the student is guided to listen out for particular information; if after, then he should, provided he has understood the text, have no trouble recalling the answers. General questions, demanding global comprehension of an entire text, must, of course be asked at the beginning or at the end (see *Summarizing*).

Some suggested books of listening passages followed by comprehension questions can be found in the *Bibliography*.

Predictions

When we hear the first part of an utterance, we may be able to guess the exact meaning, if not the exact words, of its continuation. For example, it is fairly obvious that the continuation of this: 'Do you think on the whole that people talk to each other more in the country . . .' is 'than in the town'. But more often the prediction is relatively vague. How, for example, will this finish: 'It all boils down to one thing . . .'? We cannot know the exact proposition that is to come, because we do not know the context – and even if we did, we could probably only make a rough guess. But we do know that what is coming is likely to be an emphatic statement of fact; and this kind of knowledge is perhaps hardly less useful than the more exact kind illustrated above.

The grounds given within the initial part of an utterance for prediction of certain kinds of continuations may be of various kinds. Here is a summary of some of the main types I have found; the exactness of the predictions possible decreases as the list goes on.

First, there are of course the stock formulae of the language: the clichés, idioms, quotations and proverbs which are known so widely that having heard the first half, most of us can easily predict the second. In fact, in many cases the native speaker may only say the first few words, relying on his hearer to understand the rest by himself:

    'Many hands . . .' ('make light work.')
    'The proof of the pudding . . .' ('is in the eating.')
    'No smoke . . .' ('without a fire.')

Second, stress on a particular word in the first part of an utterance is often explained or clarified by a comment in the second:

    'She wore a RED dress . . .' ('she didn't wear a blue one.')
    'I didn't see HARRY . . .' ('I saw Tom.')

Third, the logical relationship between the first part of an utterance and the second is often signalled by a conjunction: 'because' indicates a following reason, 'in order to' a purpose, 'but' or 'however' a contrast or opposition, and so on:

'One or two of the people you got talking to, but generally . . .' ('you didn't.')

'I like him because . . .' ('he's always ready with a smile.')

Sometimes there are conjunctions that occur in spaced pairs, so that if we hear the first one we can look forward to the occurrence of the second:

'Not only must you know how to answer the questions correctly . . .' ('but also . . .')

Fourth, there is the construction where the speaker proclaims in advance the kind of thing he is going to say:

'The question is . . .' (*question*)

'There are two ways of doing that . . .' (*two suggestions*)

Last, rhetorical questions or bald, brief statements, particularly in the negative, are often followed by answers, or amplification in the form of reasons, examples or explanations:

'Everything's changed . . .' (*examples*)

'I don't agree . . .' (*reasons*)

If the teacher has available a number of such beginnings-with-continuations (further examples are given below), then she can use them to give various types of practice. The simplest is to give the first part, pause to give students a chance to think forward, and then give the second. This simply helps them to focus on predicting, and gives immediate feedback. Then they can try matching exercises: fitting the right continuation to the right beginning. Perhaps the easiest way to present this is in a multiple-choice format, where the 'stem' is spoken and the options written:

He was holding TILLIE by the hand
a) not by the foot.
b) not Rachel.
c) but he isn't now.
d) not pulling her.

Finally, students can simply guess the possible continuation of the extract they hear. The teacher has to be very clear in her mind here about what is acceptable and what is not; in many cases there is a very wide range of possibilities. The material can be presented as discrete items, like those listed below; or it can take the form of one long recorded passage which the teacher can simply stop at specific points in order to ask the students to say what they think might be coming next. In this case, of course, they have a much wider context to help them guess. An example of such a passage is also given below, with asterisks to show points at which stops might be made. (I have given no examples of idioms or proverbs. Obviously there is no point in doing prediction exercises on these before students have acquired an extensive vocabulary of them by heart. For this the teacher may find helpful the books recommended in the *Bibliography* under the heading *Idioms and proverbs.*)

In general, as I have said, prediction exercises are suitable for advanced learners – hence the relative difficulty of the English of most of the examples suggested here. The latter are taken from recordings of authentic discourse from various sources, and I have given the actual continuations as they occurred in the original. Where appropriate I have added in italics a description of the kind of sentence that should be considered acceptable. This, of course, is meant only as a guide to the teacher; students do not need to be able to give such definitions, but simply to suggest examples of appropriate continuations to each beginning. In all cases the teacher should be as flexible as possible in assessing student responses:

It was going to be THIS weekend . . . (and now it's going to be next).
I probably won't be here on WEDNESDAY . . . (but anyway, I'll see you on Saturday, O.K.?)
HE doesn't make the bed . . . (his wife makes the bed).
My MOTHER'S family is from the north of England . . . (my father's is from Scotland).
I USED to go into town every day . . . (but now I don't).
That I'm not sure about yet because . . . (I've got to find out about train times). (*reason*)
I think that the National Health Service is a wonderful idea except that . . . (they can't cope with the number of people). (*reservation*)
There's lots of things I miss from home, but . . . (there's a lot of things I do like here). (*contrast, compensation*)
As well as beating the other yachts, 'Heath's Condor' . . . (also beat . . .)
One moment you'll be sitting quietly watching television . . . (and the next . . .)
I have a theory that . . . (one should eat alternately liquid and solid meals). (*a hypothesis*)
Well, you see, we've got an alternative . . . (we can go on the A417 to the M50). (*a possibility*)
I think the reason is that . . . (in Trinidad everyone participates). (*a reason*)
He didn't seem to mind . . . (Why should he? Really? He seemed to take it quite well). (*amplification*)
Don't worry . . . (I think he took it all in good part). (*justification*)
Not very long . . . (I suppose about a minute or two). (*amplification*)
How does he know? . . . (I'll tell you. He knows . . .) (*answer*)

P: . . . Isn't that right that you said the other day, or recently anyway, that you think London's changed so much that it's . . . you'd rather not come up here?

D: Yes, yes. Having lived here for a long time, having left here in 1963, the . . er . . . places, the familiar places that I used to know, they've ☆ all changed and er . . I just don't know London any more. It's dirty, it's too crowded and I love the country having lived in the country ☆ for the last 14 or 15 years, and er . . . all the tea in China ☆ wouldn't bring me back. As Dr Johnson would say, if a man's tired of London ☆ he's tired of life, so I must be tired of life.

(From *Listen, then* by Paulette Møller and Audrey Bolliger)

Prediction can be less formally but no less effectively practised when integrated with other skills in exercises based on passages of discourse. Thus we might, for example, take the passage given on p. 131 and stop at certain points to let students say what they think is coming next. After the half-sentence 'It's just as well, perhaps . . .' students might guess that a justification for the system is coming up. Or after the words 'Many animals have a natural control system which . . .' they might expect to hear what the function of the control system is, and might even be able to define it. Such quick prediction practice can be given casually and frequently within exercises whose main objective is other kinds of listening; the students are thus constantly re-minded of the need to think forward and encouraged – we hope – to make a habit of it.

Filling gaps

In these exercises students are asked to fill in missing phrases or sentences using hints given both before and after the gap; they must not only predict but also reconstruct in retrospect.

One quite well-known exercise is based on the one-sided conversation. The students hear only the speeches of one of the participants and are asked to reconstruct those of the other. These can be fairly obvious:

A: Hallo, Barbara!
B:
A: I'm fine, thank you. And you?
B:
A: Oh, I'm sorry to hear that. Have you seen the doctor?
B:
A: Well, you really ought to go, you know. Mustn't neglect yourself.

or they can be more open-ended, so that various different

responses might fit the empty slots and there is room for imagination:

A: Hi, what did you want to ask me?
B:
A: Yes, I'd love to come. Thanks for asking me. Where is it?
B:
A: I'll be there. Can I help in any way?
B:
A: O.K., I'll try to do that.

Such exercises can be presented as telephone conversations, where an eavesdropper naturally hears only one speaker. The whole sequence of heard responses should be played through once or twice to give the students an idea of the context and general direction of the conversation. Then it can be stopped at each gap to give them a chance to call out or jot down possible fillers.

Alternatively, if students are reasonably quick readers, the exercise can be based on multiple-choice questions: students listen to one side of a telephone conversation, and simultaneously read through various possible responses, marking what seems to them to be the most appropriate. In order to help students scan the written material quickly enough, it is a good idea to let them read this through once before listening. Here is part of one such exercise (intermediate level):

A: Hallo. This is 24680.
B: (*Gap One*)
A: Oh hallo, I thought it might be you. How are you?
B: (*Gap Two*)
A: Oh yes, the ones from the front room I bought at the sale.
B: (*Gap Three*)
A: They really were a bargain. I've never seen such good quality at such a price . . .

Gap One a) Are you there? Is this Jane?
         b) Hello, Jane. Celia speaking.
         c) Good morning. May I help you?
Gap Two a) I'm fine. Listen, I'm phoning about those curtains you bought last week.
         b) I'm fine. I'm phoning about that new table of yours.
         c) How are you? Have you seen my new curtains?
Gap Three a) Yes, that's right, but I can't possibly come now.
          b) Yes, the ones you said were so expensive.
          c) Yes, that's right, the ones you said were so cheap.

(From an exercise suggested by a colleague, Celia Berkovitz)

Such exercises are perhaps a little tedious to compose (I have found no published ready-made ones), but they are in some ways easier to do than the open-ended ones, and lend themselves to discussion and analysis.

Passages delivered by a single speaker can also be used. But semi-formal informative passages like news reports are unsuitable – there is so much new information that it becomes extremely difficult to guess what was missing. More appropriate are informal chatty monologues that can be found in books like *Listen to this* and *Have you heard?* by Mary Underwood or *Listening to Maggie* by Lesley Gore.

One-sided conversations with ready-made gaps can be found in *Variations on a theme* by Alan Maley and Alan Duff, and also in *Dramatic monologues* by Colin Mortimer. Any passage of informal speech can, however, be used for such exercises; if it is recorded then the teacher simply turns down the volume for a short time at predecided points; if not, then she leaves gaps herself, or 'mumbles', as suggested for *aural cloze* procedures.

Here are three of the (originally full) dialogues from *Variations on a theme* presented in this way, with multiple-choice questions to follow (intermediate level):

A: But I *am* enjoying myself.
B: (*Gap One*)
A: I'm concentrating, that's all.
B: (*Gap Two*)
A: No, let's go on. It's great.
B: (*Gap Three*)

Gap One   a) Then why are you smiling?
            b) You don't look like it.
            c) Good, so am I.
Gap Two   a) Don't you want to stop for a while?
            b) Why don't we go on for a bit?
            c) Great here, isn't it?
Gap Three a) O.K. then, we'll stop.
            b) Right, we'll have something to drink.
            c) Alright then, on we go.

A: When did he leave?
B: (*Gap One*)
A: Did you check that he had left?
B: (*Gap Two*)
A: Then he must be on his way.
B: (*Gap Three*)
A: Well, where is he then? We can't wait any longer.

Gap One   a) At eight o'clock.
            b) A second ago.
            c) Tomorrow.

Gap Two   a) No, I didn't.
             b) No, I'll go and do it now.
             c) Yes, I phoned two hours ago.
Gap Three a) But if he left at eight he would have arrived by now.
             b) I think he must have had an accident.
             c) But if he left at eight he couldn't have got here by now.

A: Phil?
B: (*Gap One*)
A: Oh, I'm sorry. Is Phil in, do you know?
B: (*Gap Two*)
A: I see. When's he coming back then?
B: (*Gap Three*)
A: Mind if I leave a message?

Gap One   a) Yes, speaking.
             b) No, Doris.
             c) What did you say?
Gap Two   a) Yes, I'll call him.
             b) Yes, but he's asleep.
             c) Yes I do. No he isn't.
Gap Three a) No idea.
             b) Don't know. Bye.
             c) Yes, here he is.

Summarizing

But in real life we seldom stop long enough to define for ourselves exactly what the word or sentence was that was missing. We simply guess its approximate meaning without formulating words, in order to get a general idea of the gist of the entire utterance. At the same time we have to be able to ignore or 'skim' other spoken information which we *can* understand but do not need to. Perhaps the best way for us to give students practice in both these skills together (coping with incomprehensible 'noise' and 'skimming' what is redundant) is to ask them to summarize the main points of a given text, either orally or in writing.

We can simply ask for a single sentence or phrase which sums up a passage, in the shape of a possible title. Thus we might call the 'marmoset' passage on p. 131 'The social organization of marmosets' or 'Reproductive habits of marmosets' or, more easily, 'How marmosets live together and have babies'. If the material is in dialogue form, students might be asked to define in one sentence what one (or both) of the participants is saying. In the last dialogue quoted above, for example, a summary of A's speeches might be 'I want to get in touch with Phil'.

Such exercises can be presented in a more structured way. Instead of just asking for a summary we can give a guiding question at the outset which is in fact a request for a summary, but expressed in such a way as to guide the listeners towards what they need to know. Such a question also helps to give some sort of preparation for content so that the hearers know what to expect. But it must be phrased carefully so that it gives this kind of preparation without giving away the essential argument: it should supply the general topic (or situation) without revealing what is actually said about it. For example, instead of asking students about the passage given below 'What is this all about?', we might ask something like 'What sort of publicity does the contraceptive pill often get in the newspapers, and what effect does such publicity have on women readers?' (advanced level):

. . . I mean, there is just so much said about things, you know, such as the pill, that I don't wonder that most women are very confused and quite frightened about it, but in fact um . . . they're often . . . um, you know, there are many sides to the argument. For instance I believe there are more deaths from . . . er . . . premature births and difficult births than there are from . . . er . . . from people dying from cancer caused purely by the pill, and these sort of facts never get into the newspaper; and I can remember reading a very sort of inflammatory headline in one newspaper about the . . . the problems caused by the pill, and unfortunately it was precisely the newspaper that would get to the m . . . majority of readers and it was precisely the newspaper that should have been slightly more reassuring about something like that . . . er . . . I think it's disastrous . . .

(From *Points overheard* by Matthew Bennett)

In another even more structured summarizing exercise students are given several possible summary-sentences and asked to say which of them fits a heard text. For example, they may have a set of newspaper headlines to match with one or more items of a news broadcast.

Note-taking is another summarizing activity that is very important as a skill in itself, particularly for students who need their English for study purposes. In this case, lecture-type material is most appropriate. Notes can be made in the native language if writing-speed is a problem, though on the whole students at a level to do exercises like these are also capable of making notes in English – indeed they may find it quicker and more convenient to do so than to translate back into their own language.

The passages used for this type of exercise need not of course be entirely comprehensible to the class. Indeed, it is important for learners to have plenty of practice in getting at the gist of material whose language is partially incomprehensible either because it is inaudible or because it is simply too difficult. One technique is simply to obliterate parts of an otherwise straightforward listening passage, and ask students to do their summary on the basis of what remains. If the material is recorded it is quite easy to make gaps by turning down the volume occasionally. This technique can be expanded into an exercise like that suggested by Alan Maley, called 'Patchwork listening' ('The teaching of listening comprehension skills', *Modern English Teacher* 6:3). The first time they hear the partially obliterated passage students note down whatever information they can. The second time the teacher turns down the volume at different points, so that much of what was missing the first time can now be filled in, or previous guesses verified. This process can continue until the students have full notes or a final summary; and the full passage may or may not be played back at the end.

Alternatively students can be asked to summarize passages whose language is largely above their level. For intermediate classes upwards, ungraded 'authentic' material can often be used. At the same time we must make sure it is not *too* difficult. If students fail to pick up the gist of a passage, they may be discouraged and less likely to try again. The teacher must make sure that the passage she is using contains at least some clearly enunciated utterances within the level of the class that they will be able to catch and understand and that include some key information. Authentic spontaneous speech is characterized by such variation, and it is common to find slow or simple utterances interspersed with fast or complex ones – unlike spoken prose, which is more uniform. But all types of discourse can and should be used, whether of informal or formal style. The passage should also not be too long: about a minute or two of this kind of listening is plenty for an intermediate-level class.

Passages suitable for summarizing can be taken from most listening comprehension books, but should be carefully selected. Monologue is more straightforward to summarize than dialogue, and exposition is better than narrative, instructions or description. Some excellent material devised specifically for note-taking and summarizing can be found in *Note-taking practice* by Donn Byrne and *Listening and note-taking* by Nicholas Ferguson and Máire O'Reilly.

5.4 Listening as a basis for study and discussion

In this last section most of the exercises entail extensive discussion and the tasks are on the whole more intellectually demanding than those of previous sections. The listening may take a relatively short time, but it serves as the basis and starting-point for each exercise. The students are expected not only to understand the heard material but also to be able to compare or collate its different parts or aspects, analyse, interpret, evaluate and reason from it. These kinds of activity are carried out typically through group discussions and may be summarized in essay form.

Problem-solving

In these exercises students hear all the information relevant to a particular problem and then set themselves to solve it, either individually or through group discussion. They will probably need to hear the information two or three times at first in order to master the details; they may be allowed to hear it again in the course of the solving process.

Not all types of problems are suitable for listening comprehension activities, and the teacher should therefore select them carefully. The logical or semi-mathematical puzzles known as 'brain-teasers' for instance are not usually easily adapted for our purposes. Their actual text is usually quite short and therefore does not give much to listen to; more important, it is very difficult to retain in one's head all the 'bits' of data in such puzzles after only a couple of hearings, let alone use them to work out a logical solution.

In order to be suitable for aural comprehension exercises the problem should be described in such a way as to be easily grasped and remembered. This means that it should not be stated as a list of disconnected facts, but as one coherent whole whose various components are connected with one another and easily remembered by association. The different pieces of information that will need to be recalled should be given at length with plenty of emphasis, redundancy and repetition to allow hearers to absorb them at their leisure; and their relevance to the central problem should be consistently clear.

Where such a problem can be based on a graphic representation of some sort, this also helps hearers to grasp it more easily. Supposing, for example, we take the second zoo exercise described on pp. 110–11. In its original form, hearers were given an account of the changes and asked to mark them in. Here, however, we would give them not the changes themselves but the various problematic situations that led up to them, and it would be up to the students to decide what to do (intermediate level):

A: Well, Mr Jones, how are things in the zoo?

B: All right, on the whole, but there are one or two minor problems.

A: If you mean the two empty enclosures – that doesn't matter, we can leave them empty for the time being.

B: No, I wasn't thinking of them particularly, though I'd like to fill at least one of them if I could. No, there are some other things. You remember those two giraffes we have by the entrance?

A: Yes, what's the matter with them, they look healthy enough to me?

B: Oh, they're healthy enough, nothing the matter with them. But we've been offered two more young giraffes at a very reasonable price, and I've decided to buy them.

A: Fine, what's wrong with that? The old giraffes will be glad of some company.

B: Yes, but it means we'll have to move them, and I don't know where to, that enclosure isn't big enough for four giraffes. Then there are complaints about the lions.

A: The lions? One died recently didn't he? So there are only two. What are they doing, roaring too much?

B: Not exactly, but they're just opposite the entrance, and apparently some of the children find them a bit scaring to face as they come in. I've had two or three letters from parents.

A: So that means moving them too.

B: Mmm. Then there's the problem of the pelicans and the llamas.

A: Yes, I noticed the llamas look a bit off-colour, and they're losing weight. And the pelicans too are behaving oddly. Why do you think that is?

B: I have an idea we shouldn't have put the llamas next to the tiger or the pelicans by the fox. You see, both tigers and foxes are predators, and you can't blame creatures like llamas and pelicans for getting a bit alarmed.

A: Makes sense. Well, we could sell the fox after all – London Zoo have been trying to buy him off us for months – quite a good offer they're making.

B: As far as the pelicans are concerned, I think the monkeys are also a bit disturbing – they do make such a noise.

A: Plenty of problems, I see: giraffes, lions, pelicans, llamas. Any bright side?

B: Oh yes, I forgot to say – the people who sold us those giraffes have also offered us two elephants and three small deer. We've always wanted elephants, and I'm sure we can fit the deer in somewhere.

A: Go ahead, buy and sell as you see fit, Mr Jones, and make any other changes you feel necessary. I have the fullest confidence in your judgement.

If students, while listening, have before them the filled-in zoo plan as shown in Fig. 25c, they will be able to follow the description of the problems with no difficulty; the plan will also help them to recall the details later and work out a solution. Further suggestions are noted at the end of this section.

Such problems are more or less open-ended. The teacher may – and should – have a suggested solution of her own ready to present as one feasible answer; but many variations are possible, so that there is plenty of room for discussion.

Other types of problems that are easily adapted for use in listening comprehension activites are personal problems based on dilemmas of conscience or emotion. The listening passage could be someone consulting a doctor or psychiatrist, or a discussion between two friends or husband and wife; or it could be a monologue – someone describing his own or someone else's situation. Here is an example (intermediate level):

Well, I suppose he's what you'd call a good husband, but still I'm thinking of leaving him. I've thought of it often before, but there were always the children. But now Effie's been married for two years and moved away, and Keith's just gone off to university, so what's the point in staying together? Just habit, I suppose. Oh, it's not that he ill-treats me or anything, but we just haven't anything in common, we don't *do* anything together. He neglects me all the time, always has, except the first two years we were married, before the kids arrived. Then we had a great time – parties, walking, going to concerts and films, meeting friends or just talking together . . . but then there were the children and we moved into a bigger house and he got a better job, and there just wasn't time. I must say for myself, I've been a good mother and housewife, he can't complain on that score, didn't think of myself at all, completely dedicated to looking after the children and the house I was. You can see for yourself what a lovely house we have, and it's well-kept, isn't it? Yes, well, I used to get some satisfaction out of that, but now the children are gone and he spends most of his time out, there doesn't seem much point. We hardly talk any more, I'm just the cook and housekeeper. He's out at work or with his friends, comes home to eat and sleep. I don't know if he's ever been unfaithful, but I shouldn't be surprised. I'm sick of the house and I'm sick of him and I want to get out, but where could I go? I'm sure Effie doesn't want me, she made it clear she was only too glad to move away, and I've no training to do any kind of job. But I'm only forty-four, there must be some way . . .

Students can be asked to listen, discuss and suggest what the speaker might do.

A third kind of problem that can be used is one based on a detective story: the kind where you listen to the details of a crime (usually a murder) and try to guess who is guilty, or how the Great Detective knows that X is guilty. Such stories can be read aloud as they stand; alternatively, with a short tale like the example given below, the teacher should be able fairly easily to memorize the main details and re-improvise:

'My dearest Tessie!' sobbed Jack Hurst as he collapsed into a chair by the lifeless body of his wife. 'Why did you do it, oh why did you do it?'

The Great Detective surveyed the scene. The body of Tess Hurst lay on the bed, a red bullet-hole in her left temple. Her left hand, still holding the gun, lay on her breast.

'We had just come back from Lady F's party,' groaned Jack Hurst.

'Is that the wife of Lord F the millionaire?'

'Yes. He's my boss. We'd been drinking a lot . . . we were quarrelling . . . Tess thought I was having an affair with Lord F's daughter. "If you don't leave her I'll kill myself," she said. She took the gun and lay down as you see her and put the gun to her head. I didn't believe her . . . I thought she was just being melodramatic. I left the room. And then . . .'

'Mr Hurst,' said the Great Detective. 'Did you touch or move the body in any way after the shot was fired?'

'No, no!' said Jack Hurst. 'I found her as you see her.'

'You are under arrest,' said the Great Detective. 'You murdered your wife in order to marry the rich Miss F.'

How did he know?

(*Solution*: The woman's hand holding the gun could not have fallen naturally onto her breast if she committed suicide by shooting herself in the temple.)

Short detective stories like these can be found in the book *Minute mysteries* by Austin Ripley. Ideas for personal problems can be found in the agony columns of women's magazines, and described in her own words by the teacher; an additional source is Michael Ockenden's *Talking points*.

As to the problems based on visual materials: here are some notes to serve as bases for the description of problems connected with maps and plans in this book:

The island (Fig. 5)
– Expanding population: but nowhere to live, no power source, no jobs.
– Many tourists: but no hotels, and beauty spots being ruined.

The town (Fig. 6)
– Want to build hotel, old people's home, multi-storey car park, petrol station, supermarket.
  Conditions: hotel – not too central
        petrol station – on main road
        old people's home – quiet

supermarket – not too far from shops
car park – not too far from shops

The shopping centre (Fig. 25e)
- Rosemary went bankrupt – but Sheila doing very well.
- Tony and Ella quarrelled.
- Benny and Carole married.
- Jack died.
- Need new washroom.

The nursing home (Fig. 25f)
- Mr Bingley died, Miss Baker got well.
- Rich Mr Toms wants enlarged room.
- Two new patients.
- TV room too small.
- Money available for building/improvements.

The school (Fig. 25g)
- Separate block has been built for Classes 1 and 2.
- Need for bigger staffroom.
- Need for small remedial teaching room, music room.
- Need for hall with small stage.

Jigsaw listening

In *Jigsaw listening* different groups of students listen to different but connected passages, each of which supplies some part of what they need to know. They then come together to exchange and pool their information and are thereby enabled to reconstruct a complete picture of a situation, or perform a task. In other words, the listening comprehension functions as a basis for various other linguistic/intellectual activities: paraphrasing and summarizing the heard information for transmission to others; discussing and organizing it into coherent form; applying the results in order to solve a problem. The different passages may simply complement one another, or there may be contradictions or inconsistencies to be resolved.

Such exercises are attractive and fun to do. But they do have some drawbacks which must be taken into account. The fact that in most cases two or three different recordings have to be listened to by two or three different groups simultaneously means that the teacher has to acquire the requisite number of tapes and recordings. If she has a ready-made recording then she may need to re-record parts of it onto other cassettes in order to play the different extracts at the same time. If she only has one recorder and tape, she may ask her groups to hear their extracts in sequence instead of simultaneously, in which case she has to think how to occupy groups who are waiting for their turn to listen, or for others to finish. Then there is the problem of disturbance. In a medium-sized classroom it may be difficult to concentrate on one recording when two others are being played in the background, or to concentrate on other occupations when a nearby group is listening to its recording. The solution is to use different rooms, or two rooms and a corridor – but this is not always possible. Or one or two of the extracts may be presented in written instead of spoken form; but then the exercise loses much of its value as a listening exercise.

Thus these exercises, though they provide effective language practice and are highly motivating, are likely to be used less than the more easily prepared and administered ones described in other sections.

Full texts of such exercises are far too long to be exemplified here; all examples of listening passages are therefore given as condensed extracts, whose purpose is simply to illustrate the ways different kinds of information can be presented and collated; they are not meant to be administered in the classroom as they stand.

COMPLEMENTARY TEXTS

In these exercises there is no conflict between the different texts; all the students have to do is collate the information from the different sources. For this it is simplest if students have a grid or other visual framework on which they can note down what they hear. They can then use this to help them transmit the information to others and can add to it what they hear in return.

The two examples below are based loosely on exercises given in *Listening links* by Marion Geddes and Gill Sturtridge. The first is based on personal details, rather like those used in *Grids*, pp. 116–21; information given in the three extracts can be combined to fill a grid like Fig. 32a:

Fig. 32a

Name				
Profession				
Address				
Age				
Appearance				

Extract 1

Pat: Do you know those four people over there by any chance?

Jon: I know the old man with the beard, Mr Sutton. He's headmaster of the local school and lives here in Cheston. I think the younger man's also a teacher in the school, I've seen him around, the one that's talking to the doctor.

Extract 2

Jason: Do introduce me to that attractive girl talking to old Mr Sutton – who is she?

Elsa: No luck, Jason, she's married, that's her husband, the tall man next to her. Name of Smith.

Jason: She looks too young to be married.

Elsa: Rose? She's twenty-two, we were at school together. She works as a secretary in her husband's school – they live quite near here.

Extract 3

Grandma: Thelma, do go and ask that nice Dr Thorndike if she'd come and talk to me for a while.

Thelma: All right, Grandma, which one is she?

Grandma: She's that middle-aged, very well-dressed lady standing over there talking to Mr Smith. She lives in London and doesn't come down here very often, so I'd love to have a chat with her.

Those hearing the first extract would be able to fill in all the details about Mr Sutton and one or two about the others. Those listening to the second would find out about Rose Smith and her husband; and the third about Dr Thorndike. By pooling their information they will be able to fill in the grid as illustrated in Fig. 32b.

Similarly, pictures and maps can be drawn according to various descriptions, 'identikit' sketches assembled through the evidence of different witnesses, Lego models built, family trees made up, stories pieced together and so on.

Fig. 32b

Name	Mr Sutton	Mr Smith	Rose Smith	Dr Thorndike
Profession	headmaster	teacher	secretary	doctor
Address	Cheston	near here (Cheston?)	near here (Cheston?)	London
Age	old	young	22	middle-aged
Appearance	bearded	tall	attractive, young-looking	well-dressed

But these exercises need not end with the simple collation of isolated facts in written or graphic form. The information can become a basis for lively discussion. Take, for example the following exercise, where three groups, each representing one of three future flat-mates, have to fill in details of a flat they hear about and might rent, together with their own personal needs and tastes (Fig. 33). When the three groups come together to pool their information they then have to decide which flat they are in fact going to take (advanced level):

Extract 1

John: Hallo, Nora? I heard about a flat that might interest you girls. It's near the central bus station on the main road and quite reasonable, about £25 rent. The only snag is it's only got two bedrooms . . . but I expect two of you could share.

Nora: Well, as long as it isn't me. I've got to have my privacy and besides I'd be working at home mostly and would need to use my bedroom as a studio as well. Canvases and paints take up room. Any other details?

John: Yes, it's got a very big and well-equipped kitchen apparently, and I know you like cooking, so that's another point in its favour. And a smallish sitting-room.

Extract 2

Peter: Jean, darling, there's this fantastic flat I heard about going for almost nothing – £10 a week.

Jean: Well, thank goodness for that, I can't afford very much on my grant. What are the details? What's the snag?

Peter: Well, it's a bit dilapidated, needs redecorating, but I'm sure your artist friend Nora could organize that side of things. Not much there in the way of furniture yet either.

Jean: What else? Is it near a bus stop?

Peter: About five minutes' walk. It backs onto the school where Alice teaches, so it might be a bit noisy during the day.

Jean: How many bedrooms?

Peter: Three – so you won't need to share and we can have some privacy when I come over.

Extract 3

Simon: Alice, some friends of mine have just vacated this flat, it might be just what you and Jean and Nora are looking for. Three bedrooms and a very quiet location.

Alice: Well, that's important, I can't bear noise. What's the rent?

Simon: About £30 I think. Rather a strict landlady, but she maintains the house perfectly and the flat is beautifully furnished.

Alice: Where is it?

Simon: Five minutes' bus ride from the school, near Jean's college. There's a bus-stop just outside the house. But let me know quickly if you want it, or it'll be taken.

	Nora and the flat she heard about	Jean and the flat she heard about	Alice and the flat she heard about
Location	near bus station, on main road	near Alice's school	quiet, 5 minutes from school, near college
Nearness to bus route	near bus station	5 minutes' walk from bus-stop	bus-stop outside house
Rent	£25	£10	£30
Number of bedrooms	2	3	3
Other details	big, well-equipped kitchen	needs redecorating and furnishing, might be noisy	quiet, strict landlady, well-maintained
My needs and tastes	need privacy and to use bedroom as studio	can't afford much rent	don't like noise

Fig. 33

All these kinds of passages can, of course, be used as bases for simple grid-filling exercises if all the students hear all the extracts. But the activity is more interesting if done in 'jigsaw' fashion as suggested here. In another variation, three groups listen to the different extracts simultaneously, and then *redivide* into other groups, each of which has at least one representative from the original ones, to compare their information and work out their conclusions. They may re-form into the original groups once or twice during the discussion in order to listen to their extracts again. In this way there will be far more participation in the discussions; but, as with almost any type of group work, one group may finish long before the others, so the teacher should have some reserve occupation ready, which can be a continuation of the task: writing out the conclusions as a composition for example.

CONFLICTING VERSIONS

In a more demanding version of such exercises the students have to evaluate information from various sources, sometimes conflicting, in order to formulate a coherent version of a situation or solve a problem. The students will often have to take notes and decide on a solution together through group or class discussion.

In the following exercise some information is given which appears to imply some present situation (for instance, the fact that Alfred and Esther had a wedding implies that they are married), only to be superseded by some other fact (that Esther is divorced). The students have to decide which is the more up-to-date information and draw the conclusion. The language is at intermediate to advanced level:

Extract 1
Now that was a lovely wedding, remember? Alfred and Esther's? Of course they were far too young to get married, but it was so romantic. And the atmosphere was catching . . . at least two other couples got engaged at that wedding. Remember Glenda? Beautiful girl, Glenda. She caught Esther's bouquet, and that rather serious young man Bob proposed to her on the spot! Frances also got engaged the same day, don't remember the young man's name. But that ended sadly, the husband was killed three years ago . . . Hope Frances is making out all right, I've rather lost touch with her. Glad *I* never got married!

Extract 2
Isn't that Glenda's little girl Hettie? What a sweet little thing, so lively and full of laughs, just like her father. How old is she now, seven, eight? Anyhow, she was born the year Frances and Chuck got married. I wonder how they are, haven't seen them for years. One never knows with marriages these days. I hear Esther got divorced a couple of years ago, *and* there were two children. Always said that wouldn't work. Best to stay single, that's what I say.

Extract 3
That Dick, always joking, you never know when to take him seriously. But I must say he has a lovely little daughter and an attractive wife. I met them a few months ago at Frances and Alfred's housewarming party. Lovely house up on Secombe Avenue. Bob was there too, I was glad to see he was married at last. He had lots of affairs when he was younger, some of them quite serious, but none of them ever worked out. Now I gather he's married Alfred's ex – but they all seem to be on good terms, and the children are fine. But of course you never know these days.

(The solution is shown in Fig. 34.)

In the two following examples, there are actual contradictions or inconsistencies, so that the students have to work out who is lying, exaggerating or mistaken before they can solve the problem. In the detective problem given the students first read the police report and then listen to the spoken evidence of the three witnesses. They compare the various accounts and try to

Name	Married	Children	What happened?	Married (2nd time)
Alfred	Esther	2	divorced	Frances
Esther	Alfred	2	divorced	Bob
Glenda	Dick	1		
Bob	Esther			
Frances	Chuck		Chuck died	Alfred
Chuck	Frances		died	
Dick	Glenda	1		

Fig. 34

draw some conclusions as to how the theft was done and who did it:

Police report

Mr Brown telephoned us at 11.10 p.m. on Thursday 12 June to report the theft of some silver from his house. The silver, consisting of some seventy items and weighing about fifty kilos, had been kept in two cabinets in the dining-room. The window of this room, which looked out onto the lawn at the back of the house, had been forced open, and there were some signs that the flower-bed immediately beneath it had been recently trampled on. The cabinets had been forced open and badly scratched and dirtied in the process, but otherwise the room was neat and clean, obviously untouched.

Mr Brown's evidence

We left home at about seven to have dinner with friends, leaving the house locked and with strict instructions to the baby-sitter to let no one in. We spent the evening at our friends' and had expected to be home by about ten, but a violent rainstorm delayed us, and we didn't leave our friends' home until about ten-thirty, getting home about eleven.

Mrs Brown's evidence

The first thing we noticed as we approached the house was the open window. We rushed into the dining-room to find the silver gone and immediately telephoned the police. We told Nora what had happened and sent her home. This morning we notified the insurance company; but these things were of sentimental value no money can replace.

Nora's evidence (the baby-sitter, aged fourteen)
I was watching television in the nursery all evening. The baby slept well the whole time. I didn't hear anyone in the house – but that's not surprising as the television was on and it was raining most of the time. I didn't even hear the Browns come in until they actually opened the nursery door. I knew nothing about the theft, only heard about it the next day when I read about it in the local paper.

(*Solution*: This is obviously an inside job, otherwise there would have been mud on the dining-room floor. Either Mrs Brown or Nora is lying about whether Nora was told about the theft immediately. It would seem unlikely that a fourteen-year-old girl could cope with fifty kilos of silver, or know how to dispose of it. Moreover, Mrs Brown must be lying when she says they saw the window was open as they approached the house . . . the window was at the *back* of the house. The Browns probably staged the theft in order to get the insurance money without losing the silver.)

But conflicting accounts of a single situation do not always arise through the fact that one person is deliberately lying. More often one version may be twisted or exaggerated because of the attitude of the person describing it; in this way discrepancies arise that are sometimes just as dramatic as those deriving from lies, and are very revealing about the feelings of the people involved. If for example we let students listen to two or more accounts of a personal or social problem, then that problem may or may not be more easily solved, but it will certainly be more challenging and interesting to tackle. Here is an example (intermediate level):

The Son
I don't know what to do about my mother. She is always criticizing me – the way I dress, the way I speak or look . . . I can't even read a book without her interrupting me to ask what it's about and tell me whether I should be reading it or not, and why. And of course every moment of my time away from her has to be accounted for . . . I try to tell her to stop interfering with my life, but it doesn't seem to help. And I've no one to advise me, my father is dead and I have no brothers or sisters. It's not as if my mother has any worries; we're fairly well off and she doesn't have to work, only do the housekeeping. I've now met a wonderful girl who I want to see a lot of, but I'm afraid to bring her to the house – when she meets my mother she won't want to see me any more. I'm nineteen years old.

The Mother
What am I to do about my son Dick? He's my only child. He means such a lot to me, especially since his father died, and I have always tried to give him all I could. He has never wanted for anything money could buy, and I have given him all my love and attention. But

nowadays he answers all my affectionate enquiries rudely, or even tells me to mind my own business. I try not to show him how hurt I am by his attitude, but often I just go off and cry. Sometimes I feel he hates me; and here I am doing my best to show him how much I love him, how much I care about everything he does. I've worked so hard for him, given him so much. Is this my reward?

(Adapted from *Discussions that work* by Penny Ur)

Here of course there is no one right solution. The two groups who have heard the different versions can come together to discuss the various aspects of the problem and decide what advice they would offer the speakers.

Ready-made 'jigsaw listening' exercises can be found in *Listening links* by Marion Geddes and Gill Sturtridge; these require students to piece together items of information which do not conflict. As far as I know, there is not yet any book available which provides listening exercises involving the evaluation of conflicting or inconsistent evidence; however, some of the texts in my book *Discussions that work* under the headings *Combining versions* and *Composing letters* can be adapted for the purpose.

Interpretative listening

When we listen to someone speaking, the meaning of what they say is only one of the things we absorb – albeit in most cases the most important. We may also perceive and take into account many other things: what kind of a person the speaker is, the way he relates to his subject, his mood, his attitude to whoever he is speaking to; what is going on around and its influence on the development of the discourse; what happened to lead up to the conversation and what may happen as its result. We perceive and understand some or all of these things at the same time as we perceive and understand the explicit meaning of the speech, in a kind of ongoing intuitive mental process.

The ability to make such interpretations is one which is acquired to a greater or lesser degree by all of us at the same time as we acquire our first language, and we carry it over to our other languages as we learn them. Insofar as some socio-cultural norms may differ from language to language, there may be differences in some of the 'signals' a hearer may need to interpret in a foreign language; but I do not think that these can be systematically taught in any detail: they are too many, too subtle, too dependent on individual variation. A proper grasp of them can only be gained intuitively by actually living in the foreign-language community for some time. The classroom teacher can do little more than point out their most obvious characteristics in contrast with those of the learners' native-language environment: conventions of courtesy for example. Armed with these, the learner will be in a good position to perceive and absorb less obvious variations in socio-cultural behaviour when he actually encounters them. In any case, most of the aspects of social behaviour we are concerned with here (outward manifestations of mood and attitude for example) are to a great extent international; if they were not we would be unable to understand and appreciate foreign films, books and plays.

While in my opinion the skill of interpretative listening cannot be *taught* to any great extent, this does not mean that it cannot be used and practised in the classroom as a feature of listening activities. Some stimulating discussions can be based on the interpretation of various aspects of a heard passage that may or may not be directly concerned with its overt meaning. For this we shall need a wide variety of recordings of authentic or simulated-authentic discourse.

Students can simply be asked to identify in general who and where the speakers are, what they are talking about, and what their relationship to each other might be. This is one of the few exercises where students are given no hint beforehand as to what the content of the listening passage is going to be – they are simply exposed to it with no preparation. They can, however, be helped by being able to look at pictures of the speakers. The following extracts for example refer to the pictures shown in Fig. 1. There is only one actual speaker in each case, but the reactions of the other participant in the conversation are made fairly clear (intermediate level):

Old man, RP accent, sounding anxious
Oh no, Mr Pearce, I assure you . . . I'll make sure it doesn't happen again . . . no no . . . he's usually such an obedient dog, we've never had anything like this before . . . no please don't do that . . . I assure you . . .

Young man, American accent, music in background
Hi Johnnie, how's things? . . . You did? Hey, that's great! I'll tell the kids . . . come on over here, we'll celebrate!

Young woman, Scots accent, loud, some talking in background
What's that? Can't hear you! What . . . right, tomorrow at seven, I'll be there . . . I said I'll be there . . . I love you too . . . Bye!

After linking the speech to the picture, students could go on to discuss just why each link was made, and to talk about any other deductions they might have made: where the conversations are taking place, who the person at the other end is and what they are saying, what has just happened, what is going to happen what sort of person the speaker is, and so on.

The rather longer monologues given in Colin Mortimer's book *Dramatic monologues* are designed to be used just this way, though without visual reinforcement. Here is an example (intermediate to advanced level):

Well, sir, I know you'll think I'm crazy. After all, five years is a long time. And now that it's come, you'd think I wouldn't be able to wait. And until last night that was exactly the way I felt. But then I started thinking. Well, it isn't an ideal life – nobody'd say it is. It's very hard, and there's a lot about it that quite honestly I've found very hard to bear. But on the other hand I've got into the routine, you know: exercise in the morning; regular work in the laundry; a small allowance for cigarettes; plenty of sleep; Frank or Jim or Ted peeping through the grille, just to check. And the lads: good company you know. And I know Michael deserved everything he got – though he says he was innocent – but he's been very good to me. Excellent conversationalist. Likes to be tidy too, just as I do. We've never had an argument, let alone a fight. Look, I know there's a limit to what you can do, sir. But I was thinking: well, the day before Christmas is just a bit too much. Can't you manage just another couple of days? Nobody'll notice. Then I'll be off, of course. Two days? One day . . .?

Colin Mortimer suggests questions that might be asked after the text has been heard – but I feel that students are activated better if they work out their interpretations in free unstructured discussion in response to one general question ('Well, what did you make of all that?') or if they suggest their own questions and answer each other.

Students can, however, be asked to focus on more specific aspects of a conversation: on the transaction being carried out (teaching–learning, thanking–acknowledging and so on) or on the communicative function of the speech of one of the participants (apologizing, complaining, enquiring, and so on). Take the following authentic exchange for example (advanced level); A is a woman and speaks in RP, B is a male cockney, and there are traffic noises in the background:

A: Okay. Two there. Two to Trafalgar Square.
B: Two twelves please. Twenty-four. Thank you very much. Thank you. Okay? That's two there.
A: Thanks.
B: Thank you. I'll tell you when to get out because I . . . if you go a stop further . . .

A: Yes.
B: It's seven pence more each . . .
A: Oh I see . . .
B: Plus you have to walk all the way back again.
A: Oh that's silly.

(From *Listen, then* by Paulette Møller and Audrey Bolliger)

The transaction is obviously the buying of tickets on a bus. Communicative functions here are more difficult to analyse because really each speech needs to be related to on its own: the first is a request, the second a request followed by thanks, followed by an offer. But in other kinds of dialogues one character consistently performs one function and the other another complementary one. The dialogues in *Variations on a theme* by Alan Maley and Alan Duff are constructed like this; in this example one character is offering help and the other politely refusing it (intermediate level):

A: You seem to be having some problems.
B: It's all right, thanks, I'll manage.
A: Perhaps I could translate for you.
B: That's very kind of you, but I think I'd better explain myself.
A: Shall I ask him if he's understood you properly?
B: It's very kind of you indeed, but he knows what I want.
A: Well, if you're sure I can't help.
B: No, really. Thank you very much.

Another specific aspect that can be concentrated on is the speaker himself: what sort of a person is he? What is his mood at the time of speaking? Why? How does he feel about the person he is speaking to? About the topic? I leave the reader to make his or her own such interpretations from this extract (advanced level):

A: Well look. The thing is, I, I, look I, if, if you can be dropped this time, I, I mean we can, we can give you another chance . . .
J: Aa . . . oh!
A: later in the season.
J: Ah . . . oh no! Stuff it! I mean this is, this is stupid. I mean I've been playing as well as any other man in the team and you ought to know that, I mean, this is . . .
A: There's nothing I can do about it John, I mean.
J: Pfuf! All . . . I think your team's a . . . well it's a dead loss anyway, I've, I . . . I, I don't bloody care if I ever play for you again. Let's put it like that straight. If you want, if you want cards on the table, that's it.
A: Well, don't take it like that eh . . .?
J: No, I'm sorry, I feel this way.

(From *Learning to listen* by Alan Maley and Sandra Moulding)

Materials for these kinds of exercises must be carefully selected. Unfortunately texts given in many listening comprehension books convey very little information beyond actual semantic content. Most recordings take place against a silent and therefore totally neutral background, the participants are of indeterminate age and character, speak in a standard accent, display no emotion and are discussing a topic that has nothing to do with their situation at the time of speaking – they are rarely actually performing a significant communicative transaction. However, there are several honourable exceptions to this, books that do give material with scope for interpretative listening: the ones from which I have taken the examples above, for instance, and others such as *Listening to Maggie* by Lesley Gore and the *Listeners* series by Mary Underwood and Pauline Barr.

Evaluative and stylistic analysis

Students who are able to understand the information explicitly conveyed in a piece of heard discourse and also appreciate some of the more subtle, implicit 'messages' may go one step further and try to analyse its style and assess its impact. Thus, they discuss not only what a speaker is trying to do, but also how he is going about it, what the characteristics of his speech are, what effect these have on them as hearers. To do this they will obviously have to be highly proficient in spoken English; and they will have to engage in stylistic analysis. Quite how far a group of students is able to define and talk about the more subtle aspects of linguistic style will depend on the academic level of the class and the objectives and content of their course. But even if they have only the normal sensitivity of reasonably fluent language users, they should be able to distinguish between, for example, different registers or levels of formality, and make some comment on why a certain piece of spoken English has a certain effect. Knowledge the students may have from sources other than the heard passage itself may also be brought into play; and the whole activity will involve their feelings, attitudes, tastes and values as well as their intellectual abilities.

We therefore need a collection of sound or video recordings of all imaginable types of spoken or sung English, using a variety of voice-types, accents and background visual and aural effects. However the extracts should not be composed of language that is too difficult, specialized or exotic, nor should they be very culture-bound; they should be of a type likely to be appreciated by any reasonably well-educated student from a Western-type culture with an advanced knowledge of English and good listening comprehension. Here are some possibilities.

INTERVIEWS

Radio or television interviews with well-known or interesting personalities on topical subjects are likely to be listened to with interest. Students can then discuss the personality of the interviewee, how he expressed himself and what they think of his ideas. They may also analyse the technique of the interviewer: was he aggressive or sympathetic? Did he manage to extract the information he wanted? How far did he reveal his own opinions?

COMEDY

It is quite fun to listen to and assess the patter and jokes of solo comedians or the volley of back-chat between a team of two or more. Was it funny? Why or why not? On what was the humour based? Is there such a thing as English or American humour? What are the differences between the kind of humour expressed in the recordings and that of the students' native culture?

DRAMA

Students can listen to or watch plays on television, radio or film. Occasionally they may be able to go to the live theatre. There is plenty to criticize and discuss after seeing or hearing good drama: the play itself, its plot, themes, characters, language; the direction; the actors' performances; and, where appropriate, the lighting, scenery, special effects, camera-work.

ADVERTISING

Radio or television commercials can be recorded and played to a class. These are usually very short but have plenty to discuss in them. Do the students find the advertisement convincing or not? What effect does it try to achieve and how? What sort of image of the product does it try to project? At what kind of population is it aimed? Is it in good taste? Does it violate any kind of moral code? Does it have any aesthetic or artistic merit in itself? Is it disturbing in any way? What kinds of motivations or anxieties does it try to play on?

RHETORIC

Various kinds of rhetorical speech can be heard and discussed, chiefly with a view to analysing in what way the speaker hopes to influence his audience, how he goes about it, and to what extent he is, or is likely to be, successful. As part of the introduction to such recordings the teacher should make clear under what circumstances the speech was delivered, and to what audience – otherwise the students may not be in a position to make valid judgements. Some examples might be: orators at Speakers' Corner in Hyde Park; extracts from Winston Churchill's wartime speeches; part of an inauguration speech by a President of the United States; some of the contributions to university or school debates; broadcast appeals for contributions to charity; sermons.

POETRY

Some poetry was written to be read silently – but much was obviously meant to be listened to: old ballads, for example, or children's rhymes. Even if a poem is read silently, the reader's appreciation will be heightened by hearing a good, thoughtful recitation. Classroom discussion will centre mostly around the poem itself, and here it obviously depends on the teacher and students how they will wish to approach it: whether they prefer to emphasize the theme, imagery, language, structure, rhythm and so on – or whether they prefer to discuss all these as little as possible in order to leave the poem to make its own impact. A more sophisticated discussion can centre round the interpretation of the reader: did he understand and convey the meaning and feeling of the poem in accordance with the students' understanding of it? Where did he read particularly well or badly?

There are, of course, many other kinds of discourse that could have been discussed in this section: songs, quiz and chat shows, documentaries, news reporting, lectures, lessons, and so on. But I hope that enough examples have been given here to illustrate the possibilities. As far as I know, no ready-made anthology of such material has yet been published, but an enterprising teacher can collect her own from records, tapes, television and the radio. Some ideas on stylistic analysis of spoken material can be found in *Investigating English style* by David Crystal and Derek Davy.

A postscript: conversation

Conversation is not usually thought of as a listening exercise; and yet it is the culmination of all kinds of aural practice in that it is easily the most common context of listening activity in real life. When a foreign-language learner can keep up his end in ordinary speech transactions with native speakers, he can claim to be proficient in the oral skills. For the purposes of this book 'listening comprehension' has been treated as if it were an isolated skill – and in the classroom it can be practised as such up to a certain point; but in the long run it must obviously be integrated with active speech production. A normal member of society must both listen and be listened to, absorb the speech of others and produce his own; and the two activities are commonly practised together in the classroom. Listening within a conversation is a more complex process than listening in other situations: it is not enough just to understand what the other participants are saying; very often we use the time they are talking not only to listen but also to start formulating our own reply, and to watch out for an opportunity to cut in with it.

Routine classroom discussions or discussion-games are only partially effective in preparing a learner for the listening that occurs in real-life conversations, in that they give him practice only in talking with other learners in his class, who probably speak fairly slowly and with similar shortcomings to his own in their production of spoken English. He needs to try himself in conversation with native speakers, or at least with speakers of a high level of proficiency. If, therefore, a teacher can get such people to come into conversation classes occasionally and take part in the proceedings as members of the discussion-groups, this is all to the good. Even if no such assistants are available there is always the teacher herself. She is only one individual and cannot interact with many of her class at the same time, but she can nevertheless supply some minimal native (or near-native) speaker participation. Where a class is well organized and a teacher can afford to abandon at least in part her role as supervisor and instructor, there is a strong case for having her actually participate in discussion activities on equal terms with her students. Some ideas on the organization and content of discussions in the classroom can be found in my book *Discussions that work* and in some books of communication games, notably *Games for language learning* by Andrew Wright, David Betteridge and Michael Buckby.

Bibliography

Background reading

Brown, Gillian, *Listening to spoken English*, Longman, 1977.

Brown, Gillian, 'Understanding spoken language', *TESOL Quarterly* 12:2, 1978.

Brown, Gillian and Yule, George, *Teaching the spoken language*, Cambridge University Press, 1983.

Byrne, Donn, 'Listening comprehension', *Teaching oral English*, Longman, 1976.

Crystal, David and Davy, Derek, *Investigating English style*, Longman, 1969.

Curfs, Emile, 'Listening deserves better', *Modern English Teacher* 9:3, 1982.

Geddes, Marion, 'Listening', in K. Johnson and K. Morrow (eds.), *Communication in the classroom*, Longman, 1981.

Geddes, Marion and White, Ron, 'The use of semi-scripted simulated authentic speech and listening comprehension', *Audio-visual Language Journal* 16:3, 1978.

Littlewood, William, *Communicative language teaching*, Cambridge University Press, 1981.

Maley, Alan, 'The teaching of listening comprehension skills', *Modern English Teacher* 6:3, 1978.

Porter, Don and Roberts, Jon, 'Authentic listening activities', *English Language Teaching Journal* 36:1, 1981.

Richards, Jack C., 'Listening comprehension', *TESOL Quarterly* 17:2, 1983.

Rivers, Wilga, 'Hearing and comprehending', *Teaching foreign language skills* (revised edn.), University of Chicago Press, 1980.

Widdowson, Henry, *Teaching language as communication*, Oxford University Press, 1978.

The teaching of listening comprehension, British Council, E.L.T. Documents Special, 1981.

Listening for perception

Baker, Ann, *Ship or sheep?*, 2nd edn, Cambridge University Press, 1981.

Baker, Ann, *Tree or three?*, Cambridge University Press, 1982.

Baker, Ann, *Introducing English pronunciation*, Cambridge University Press, 1982.

Mortimer, Colin, *Elements of pronunciation*, Cambridge University Press, 1984.

Roach, Peter, *English Phonetics and Phonology*, Cambridge University Press, 1983.

Russell, Michael, *Aural tests*, Evans, 1974.
Templer, J. C., *Listening comprehension tests*, Heinemann Educational
    Books, 1971.
Templer, J. C., *Further listening comprehension tests*, Heinemann
    Educational Books, 1972.

Task-centred listening

Blundell, Lesley and Stokes, Jackie, *Task listening*, Cambridge University
    Press, 1981.
Gore, Lesley, *Listening to Maggie*, Longman, 1979.
McClintock, John and Stern, Börje, *Let's listen*, Heinemann Educational
    Books, 1974.
Maley, Alan and Moulding, Sandra, *Learning to listen*, Cambridge
    University Press, 1981.
Scott, Wendy, *Are you listening?*, Oxford University Press, 1980.
Stokes, Jacqueline St Clair, *Elementary task listening*, Cambridge
    University Press, 1984.
Underwood, Mary and Barr, Pauline, *Listeners* (series), Oxford University
    Press, 1980.

Visual materials that can be used for listening activities

Abbs, Brian and Freebairn, Ingrid, *Wall pictures for beginners of English*,
    Longman, 1977.
Byrne, Donn, *Progressive picture compositions*, Longman, 1967.
Byrne, Donn and Hall, Douglas, *Wall pictures for language practice*,
    Longman, 1976.
Byrne, Donn and Wright, Andrew, *What do you think?*, Longman, 1975.
Byrne, Donn and Wright, Andrew, *Say what you think*, Longman, 1977.
Groves, Paul, Grimshaw, Nigel and Schofield, Roy, *The Goodbodys*,
    Edward Arnold, 1976.
Harkess, Shiona and Eastwood, John, *Cue for a drill*, Oxford University
    Press, 1976.
Harkess, Shiona and Eastwood, John, *Cue for communication*, Oxford
    University Press, 1980.
Hill, L. A., *Picture composition book*, Longman, 1960.
Holden, Susan (ed), *Visual aids for classroom interaction*, Modern English
    Publications, 1978.
Maley, Alan, Duff, Alan, and Grellet, Françoise, *The mind's eye*,
    Cambridge University Press, 1980.

Story-telling

Morgan, John and Rinvolucri, Mario, *Once upon a time*, Cambridge
    University Press, 1983.

Songs

Abbs, Brian and Jones, T., *Cloudsongs*, Longman, 1977.
Abbs, Brian and York, N., *Skyhigh*, Longman, 1975.
Jones, Christopher, *Back home*, Longman, 1980.
Kingsbury, Roy, and O'Shea, Patrick, *Seasons and people and other songs*, Oxford University Press, 1979.
Wilson, Ken, *Mister Monday and other songs for the teaching of English*, Longman, 1971.
Wilson, Ken and Morrow, Keith, *Goodbye rainbow*, Longman, 1974.

Summarizing and note-taking

Byrne, Donn, *Note-taking practice*, Longman, 1978.
Ferguson, Nicholas and O'Reilly, Máire, *Listening and note-taking*, Evans, 1972.
James, K., Jordan, R. and Matthews, A, *Listening comprehension and note-taking course*, Collins, 1979.
Lynch, Tony, *Study listening*, Cambridge University Press, 1983.
Wallace, Michael J., *Study skills in English*, Cambridge University Press, 1980.
Yorkey, Michael, *Study skills*, McGraw Hill, 1970.

Listening text with comprehension questions

Black, Colin, *Advanced listening comprehension*, Evans, 1976.
Byrne, Donn, *Listening comprehension practice*, Longman, 1978.
Ferguson, Kenneth, *Listen and choose*, Evans, 1973.
Fowler, W. S., *First Certificate English 4: listening comprehension*, Nelson, 1975.
Templer, J. C., *Listening comprehension tests*, Heinemann Educational Books, 1971.
Templer, J. C., *Further listening comprehension tests*, Heinemann Educational Books, 1972.

Idioms and proverbs

Seidl, Jennifer and McMordie, W., *English idioms and how to use them*, Oxford University Press, 1978.
Wilson, F. P. (ed.), *Oxford Dictionary of English Proverbs*, Oxford University Press, 1970.

Jigsaw listening and problem-solving

Geddes, Marion and Sturtridge, Gill, *Listening links*, Heinemann Educational Books, 1979.
Methold, Kenneth, Cobb, David and Land, Geoffrey, *Puzzles for English practice*, Longman, 1979.
Ockenden, Michael, *Talking points*, Longman, 1977.
Ripley, Austin, *Minute mysteries*, Pocket Books Inc., New York, 1949.

Interpretative listening

Gore, Lesley, *Listening to Maggie*, Longman, 1979.
Maley, Alan and Duff, Alan, *Variations on a theme*, Cambridge University Press, 1978.
Møller, Paulette and Bolliger, Audrey, *Listen, then,* Munksgaard, Denmark, 1979.
Mortimer, Colin, *Dramatic monologues for listening comprehension*, Cambridge University Press, 1978.
O'Neill, Robert and Scott, Roger, *Viewpoints*, Longman, 1974.

Miscellaneous sources of further material

Bennett, Matthew, *Points overheard*, Macmillan, 1975.
Chamberlain, A. and Stenburg, K., *Play and practise,* J. Murray, 1976.
Fredrickson, Terry L., *Meeting people*, Longman, 1980.
Holden, Susan, (ed), *Teaching children*, Modern English Publications, 1980.
James, Gary, Whitley, Charles G. and Bode, Sharon, *Listening in and speaking out*, Longman, 1980.
O'Keefe, J. J., *People overheard*, Macmillan, 1975.
Underwood, Mary, *Listen to this*, 2nd edn, Oxford University Press, 1975.
Underwood, Mary, *What a story!*, Oxford University Press, 1976.
Underwood, Mary, *Have you heard?*, Oxford University Press, 1979.
Ur, Penny, *Discussions that work*, Cambridge University Press, 1981.
Webster, Megan and Castañón, Libby, *Crosstalk*, Oxford University Press, 1980.
Wright, Andrew, Betteridge, David and Buckby, Michael, *Games for language learning*, 2nd edn, Cambridge University Press, 1984.

Periodicals

Modern English Teacher, Modern English Publications.
Practical English Teacher, Mary Glasgow Publications.

Index of activities